Our Centennial Indian War
and the
Life of General Custer

The Western Frontier Library

Our Centennial Indian War *and the* Life of General Custer

By FRANCES FULLER VICTOR

Introduction by
JEROME A. GREENE

UNIVERSITY OF OKLAHOMA PRESS
Norman

Our Centennial Indian War and the Life of General Custer is Volume 68 in The Western Frontier Library.

Library of Congress Cataloging-in-Publication Data

Victor, Frances Fuller, 1826–1902

Our centennial Indian War and the life of General Custer / by Frances Fuller Victor ; introduction by Jerome A. Greene.

p. cm. — (Western frontier library ; v. 68)

Includes index.

Originally published as a concluding element of Victor's Eleven years in the Rocky Mountains and a life on the frontier, 1877.

ISBN 978-0-8061-4173-2 (hardcover : alk. paper)

1. Dakota Indians—Wars, 1876. 2. Little Bighorn, Battle of the, Mont., 1876. 3. Custer, George A. (George Armstrong), 1839–1876. I. Victor, Frances Fuller, 1826–1902. Eleven years in the Rocky mountains and life on the frontier. II. Title.

E83.876.V53 2011

973.8'2—dc22

2010030472

The paper in this book meets the guidelines for permanence and durability of the Committee on Production Guidelines for Book Longevity of the Council on Library Resources, Inc. ∞

1 2 3 4 5 6 7 8 9 10

CONTENTS

Our Centennial Indian War and the Life of General Custer

INTRODUCTION

JEROME A. GREENE

Our Centennial Indian War and the Life of General Custer, by Frances Fuller Victor, originally appeared in the spring of 1877, before the Great Sioux War had ended but after months of intensive army campaigning had forecast the conflict's inevitable conclusion. As the first book-length treatment of the war, it was a major accomplishment for its time, for it drew together, straightforwardly and comprehensively, information from diverse period sources to offer a synthesis and give meaning to the wide-ranging struggle. For contemporary readers, Frances Victor provided the sole extensive telling of the war's causes and of the actions preceding and following its climactic moment, the defeat by Lakota and Northern Cheyenne warriors of Lieutenant Colonel George Armstrong Custer and the Seventh Cavalry at the Little Bighorn River in Montana Territory on June 25–26, 1876.[1]

1. Modern treatments of aspects of the Great Sioux War of 1876–77 appear in John S. Gray, *Centennial Campaign: The Sioux War of 1876* (Fort Collins, Colo.: Old Army Press, 1976); Charles M. Robinson III, *A Good Year to Die: The Story of the Great Sioux War* (New York: Random House, 1995), and Paul L. Hedren, *Fort*

The Battle of the Little Bighorn dwarfed all other engagements of the Great Sioux War. In the public mind, the battle eventually came to represent the gist not only of that conflict but of all other Indian wars of the trans-Mississippi West. The value of *Our Centennial Indian War,* then as today, lay in its account of the episodic contest that in 1876–77 played out across the plains of Wyoming, Montana, and Dakota Territories. Along with Little Bighorn, the actions in that contest are called the Great Sioux War, to distinguish it from lesser struggles fought between troops and various groups of Sioux tribesmen during the nineteenth century. In addition, Victor included a biography of Custer, who was to white Americans of the day the most prominent luminary in the war, owing to his previous Civil War successes and his spectacular demise at the Little Bighorn.

The Great Sioux War resulted essentially from government and commercial expansion onto the northern Great Plains and opposition to it by many of the native peoples who lived there. In 1868, many Lakotas (also known as Tetons, or Western Sioux) had subscribed to a treaty made at Fort Laramie, in present Wyoming, that called on them to move to a tract in the southwestern quarter of Dakota Territory designated the Great Sioux Reservation. Many Lakotas complied with the

---

Laramie and the Great Sioux War (Norman: University of Oklahoma Press, 1998). A brief overview is in Jerome A. Greene (comp., ed.), *Battles and Skirmishes of the Great Sioux War, 1876–1877: The Military View* (Norman: University of Oklahoma Press, 1993).

stricture, but others did not. In the summer of 1873, troops accompanying survey parties of the Northern Pacific Railroad clashed with tribesmen under Sitting Bull on traditional hunting grounds along the Yellowstone River in Montana Territory. During the following year, an army expedition commanded by Custer discovered gold in the Black Hills of Dakota Territory, on part of the Indian reservation, an enterprise that further breached the treaty with the Sioux and instigated a gold rush into the region by whites. Desiring to wrest the lucrative Black Hills from the tribes, the federal government late in 1875 directed all affected Sioux onto the reservation. When the people did not respond promptly, the government turned to the army to force the issue.[2]

Our Centennial Indian War describes the military maneuvers inspired in 1876–77 to drive the Indians from their coveted lands onto the appointed reserve. The campaigns comprised Brigadier General George Crook's Big Horn Expedition, which clashed with the Indians at Powder River, Montana, in March 1876; Crook's subsequent Big Horn and Yellowstone Expedition, which resulted in his defeat by the Sioux and Northern Cheyennes at Rosebud Creek, Montana, in June; the successive campaigning of Brigadier General Alfred H. Terry, Colonel John

2. For the Yellowstone encounters, see M. John Lubetkin, *Jay Cooke's Gamble: The Northern Pacific Railroad, the Sioux, and the Panic of 1873* (Norman: University of Oklahoma Press, 2006). For the Black Hills expedition of 1874, see Ernest Grafe and Paul Horsted, *Exploring with Custer: The 1874 Black Hills Expedition* (Custer, S. Dak.: Golden Valley Press, 2002).

Gibbon, and Custer, which culminated in the army disaster (and Indian triumph) at the Little Bighorn just one week after Rosebud Creek; and the ensuing movements by Crook into Dakota Territory and the army's first registered victory over the Indian coalition at Slim Buttes, in September. Later operations included the Powder River Expedition, in which Colonel Ranald S. Mackenzie delivered a major attack on Northern Cheyennes secluded in Wyoming's Big Horn Mountains in November 1876, and Colonel Nelson A. Miles's successes against the intertribal alliance in areas adjoining the Yellowstone River through the autumn and winter of 1876–77, primarily his engagements at Cedar Creek and Wolf Mountains. In the early months of the new year, most of the disheartened Indians yielded at the Great Sioux Reservation agencies or surrendered to Miles on the Yellowstone. The killing of Crazy Horse, who had played a significant role throughout the combat, symbolically closed the war in September 1877.[3] Meanwhile,

3. Readers interested in these actions might consult the following studies for further details: J. W. Vaughn, *The Reynolds Campaign on Powder River* (Norman: University of Oklahoma Press, 1961); Neil Mangum, *Battle of the Rosebud: Prelude to the Little Bighorn* (El Segundo, Calif.: Upton and Sons, 1987); James Donovan, *A Terrible Glory: Custer and the Little Bighorn, the Last Great Battle of the American West* (New York: Little, Brown, 2008); Jerome A. Greene, *Slim Buttes, 1876: An Episode of the Great Sioux War* (Norman: University of Oklahoma Press, 1982); Jerome A. Greene, *Morning Star Dawn: The Powder River Expedition and the Northern Cheyennes, 1876* (Norman: University of Oklahoma Press, 2003); Jerome A. Greene, *Yellowstone Command: Colonel Nelson A. Miles and the Great Sioux War, 1876–1877* (Norman: University of Oklahoma Press, 2006); and Kingsley M. Bray, *Crazy Horse: A Lakota Life* (Norman: University of Oklahoma Press, 2006). For

several thousand Sioux under Sitting Bull and other leaders crossed into Canada, where they remained until 1880–81. Except for these final proceedings, which took place during the months after *Our Centennial Indian War* was published, it is this succession of events that is addressed in Victor's narrative.

Though largely unknown to readers today, Frances Fuller Victor was no novice in her field and indeed came to her topic with strong credentials as a writer and historian. She became not only the first woman to write and publish a book about Custer—preceding by eight years the publication of Elizabeth B. Custer's *Boots and Saddles*[4]—but also the first person to chronicle the broadly encompassing aspects of the Great Sioux War of 1876–77. Her book afforded readers the first inclusive treatment of the war's causes and sequential operations against the Lakota–Northern Cheyenne union, together with its then known conclusions.

Victor was born Frances Auretta Fuller in Rome, New York, on May 23, 1826, and within a few years moved with her parents and sisters to Ohio. Educated at a girls' school in Wooster, Frances at age fourteen was contributing literary pieces to the local newspaper. By her early twenties, she and her sister Metta

---

accounts by army participants in these actions, see Greene, *Battles and Skirmishes,* and for statements by Sioux and Cheyenne participants and witnesses, see Jerome A. Greene (comp., ed.), *Lakota and Cheyenne: Indian Views of the Great Sioux War, 1876–1877* (Norman: University of Oklahoma Press, 1994).

4. Elizabeth B. Custer, "*Boots and Saddles,*" *or Life in Dakota with General Custer* (New York: Harper and Brothers, 1885).

had established themselves regionally through their prose and poetry, and in 1851 they penned their first book of verse, *Poems of Sentiment and Imagination,* for which they garnered enthusiastic acclaim. Two years later Frances married Jackson Barritt of Pontiac, Michigan, and went with him to Nebraska to take up farming. But the marriage failed, and in 1859 she relocated to New York City, where she authored several well-received women's dime novels.

Three years later, Frances married Henry Clay Victor, a naval engineer, with whom she moved to California. She began publishing articles in the *Overland Monthly* and *Out West Magazine*, as well as in San Francisco and Sacramento newspapers, under the name Frances Fuller Victor. Her first significant historical essay, "Manifest Destiny in the West," appeared in 1869. The Victors relocated to Oregon, where Frances, caught up in the grandeur of the Pacific Northwest, soon focused on regional history and geography while taking an avid interest in women's causes. In Portland she met the aging mountain man Joe Meek, who inspired her book *The River of the West* (1870, 1871). It offered an epic history of the early West through Meek's adventures in the Rocky Mountains, the northern and central plains, and California and the Pacific Coast. Shortly thereafter, she published *All Over Oregon and Washington* (1872, under the pseudonym Florence Fane), a virtual handbook to the region, and *The Women's War with Whiskey; or Crusading in Portland* (1874).

In 1875, Henry Victor died in the foundering of the steamship *Pacific* near Puget Sound. Thereafter, Frances became self-supporting and consequently increasingly prolific as a writer of books and articles about the history of the Northwest. In 1878 she joined the firm of Hubert Howe Bancroft in San Francisco, contributing much of her own research in ghostwriting several volumes in the Bancroft's Works series on the history of the West, notably *History of Oregon, 1832–1847* (1886), *History of Oregon, 1848–1888* (1888), *History of Washington, Idaho and Montana, 1845–1889* (1890), and *History of Nevada, Colorado and Wyoming* (1890), and adding substantially to several others. Yet throughout her career as a writer she barely got by. She generated numerous works—over thirty-seven years she wrote eleven books, ranging from short novels to lengthy historical tomes, besides numerous articles and poems—but despite her widely respected reputation, she endured almost constant financial hardship. After completing her work with Bancroft, she returned to Oregon and wrote *Atlantis Arisen; or, Talks of a Tourist about Oregon and Washington* (1891) and *The Early Indian Wars of Oregon* (1894). A planned biography of Marcus Whitman, along with other writing projects, went unfulfilled when Victor died in a boarding house in Portland on November 14, 1902.[5]

5. Further details about Victor appear in Jim Martin, *A Bit of a Blue: The Life and Work of Frances Fuller Victor* (Salem, Ore.: Deep Well Publishing, 1992), from which I have drawn the information given here.

Frances Victor's legacy as an historian clearly derives from her studies of the history of the Pacific Northwest. Although *The River of the West* doubtless stands as her single most noted contribution, all of her historical work exhibits vivid narration, impartiality, and forthrightness in style, sometimes to the extent that it raised controversy. Her productivity as a scribe for Bancroft's monumental project, for which he alone (despite her protestations) was initially recognized, went mostly unacknowledged during her lifetime. *Our Centennial Indian War* originally saw publication only as an appendix—effectively a supplemental bonus book—to a reprint of *The River of the West,* retitled *Eleven Years in the Rocky Mountains and Life on the Frontier,* with which Victor and her publisher hoped to capitalize on public interest in the then current Sioux Indian situation. The Columbian Book Company, of Hartford, Connecticut, released the volume in 1877; a subsequent printing by R. W. Bliss and Company, also of Hartford, appeared in 1881.[6] Although sales figures for the expanded edition are presently unknown, the pronounced rarity of either printing in the antiquarian market today suggests that despite its contemporaneous treatment of the 1876–77 Indian conflict, the bolstered version did not prove an overwhelming marketing success.

6. Internal evidence suggests that the retitled edition of *The River of the West,* with *Our Centennial Indian War and the Life of General Custer* appended, appeared in the spring of 1877, soon after Crazy Horse surrendered at the Red Cloud Agency, Nebraska, and as reports initially circulated of Sitting Bull's imminent departure for Canada (see p. 105).

Victor's rendering of the Great Sioux War, assimilating Little Bighorn with surrounding events, constitutes in itself a remarkable account. She justified the addition, she said, because the conflict with the Sioux and Northern Cheyennes took place "over the identical ground where the fur-traders roamed," and the record of this Indian war would "appropriately supplement the story of the Mountain-men." (And that is where she takes up the subject in her introduction.) Augmented with the account of Custer's life, her book contained the most complete treatment of the war then available. In imparting personal estimates of Custer by his contemporaries, she included one (pp. 156–59) now known to have been contributed by fellow officer Captain William Ludlow that first appeared in the *New York Tribune.*[7] Victor's book was published after Frederick Whittaker's first full-length biography of Custer arrived late in 1876, just six months after the Little Bighorn. Whittaker took strong issue with Major Marcus A. Reno's leadership decisions at the battle, but Victor seems more charitable toward his actions, and her story of Custer's career, although concise, in that respect might be viewed as something of an antidote to Whittaker's. [8]

Throughout her book Victor drew from an array of primary materials such as government documents and reports and personal accounts in letters, and she included often lengthy

7. Robert M. Utley, *Custer and the Great Controversy: The Origin and Development of a Legend* (Los Angeles: Westerlore Press, 1962), 152.

8. Frederick Whittaker, *A Complete Life of Gen. George A. Custer* (New York: Sheldon and Company, 1876).

excerpts from these. Her narrative was smooth, dispassionate, and non-interpretive, and it generally reflected the sentiment of most white citizens of the day. Although she acknowledged that treaties and the miners' invasion of the Black Hills had wronged the Indians, she often adhered to the government line in recounting efforts to defeat the tribes; otherwise, her treatise was extremely unbiased. Nor did she theorize about events or direct blame in their outcome, especially in regard to the Battle of the Little Bighorn. Appreciably, considering the time in which *Our Centennial Indian War* was written, the book contained rare Indian perspectives of the Custer battle, particularly one by the warrior Little Buck-Elk that has evidently been overlooked and not previously published elsewhere. There is also included a substantive body of Indian testimony regarding the September 1876 councils over the sale of the Black Hills, which further promotes the book's value for modern readers. Victor's occasional references to the Indians as hostiles, though reflective of period sentiment with respect to the Sioux and Northern Cheyennes, are considered inappropriate today.

Because *Our Centennial Indian War* appeared while the combat was ongoing, not all aspects of its assorted elements were yet well known, and the book occasionally contains omissions that require explanation so that readers can understand the full scope of the conflict. Victor's discussion of causes did not acknowledge the intrusion of the Northern Pacific Railroad survey into Sioux hunting lands, which so aroused Sitting

Bull's people along the Yellowstone in the summer of 1873 and steeled them to the military incursions three years later. Nor did her narrative incorporate the skirmish at Warbonnet Creek, Nebraska, in July 1876, the first formal engagement after the Little Bighorn, in which cavalry under Colonel Wesley Merritt halted a body of Northern Cheyennes bound for the war zone. Victor made no mention of Colonel Miles's attack on Lame Deer's village in May 1877 or of the death of Crazy Horse at Camp Robinson, Nebraska, the following September, both of which events likely occurred well after her account went to press. Too, the small-scale army efforts to force scattered bodies of tribesmen into the agencies during the late summer and fall of 1877 went unrecounted in her book.[9]

Occasional inaccuracies in the narrative require correction. Regarding the account of Colonel Joseph J. Reynolds's attack on the presumed village of Crazy Horse along the Powder River on March 17, 1876 (pp. 22–25), it must be noted that the camp contained predominantly Northern Cheyennes, not Lakotas, and the Sioux leader was not present. Victor's description of the Battle of the Little Bighorn (pp. 40–60) contains a

9. See Lubetkin, *Jay Cooke's Gamble,* for details of the Northern Pacific Railroad survey operations in 1873. For Warbonnet Creek, see Paul L. Hedren, *First Scalp for Custer: The Skirmish at Warbonnet Creek, Nebraska, July 17, 1876, with a Short History of the Warbonnet Battlefield* (rev. ed., Lincoln: Nebraska State Historical Society, 2005). Final military operations in the late summer of 1877 are detailed in Jerome A. Greene, "Out with a Whimper: The Little Missouri Expedition and the Close of the Great Sioux War," *South Dakota History* 35 (Spring 2005): 1–39.

few directional errors. Her reference to the "upper ravine" denotes today's Deep Coulee, and that to the "lower ravine" pertains to Deep Ravine. Victor noted that Mark Kellogg worked for the *New York Herald* (p. 42); he actually was a correspondent for the *Bismarck Tribune* and a stringer for the New York paper. Mentions of Assistant Surgeon L. W. Lord, Lieutenant E. L. Godfrey, and George Herndon (pp. 55, 56) should accurately refer to George E. Lord, Lieutenant Edward S. Godfrey, and George Herendeen, respectively, the latter an interpreter with Major Marcus A. Reno's command. The "Gerard" and "Babtiste" (p. 74) named in reference to Lieutenant Frederick Sibley's scout in the Big Horn Mountains and the later Slim Buttes engagement (p. 79) were two of General Crook's scouts, Frank Grouard and Baptiste Pourier. The officer wounded at Slim Buttes, identified as "Lieut. Von Leuttroitz" (p. 80), was First Lieutenant Adolphus H. Von Leuttwitz. And the wagon train passing west along the Yellowstone from the Glendive Cantonment in October 1876, preceding a fight with the Sioux, was escorted by troops of the Twenty-second and Seventeenth Infantry regiments, not the Sixth Infantry, as stated (p. 82). The "Redwood" country mentioned as backdrop to Lieutenant Frank D. Baldwin's strike against Sitting Bull's people (p. 97) should correctly be the Redwater country. Finally, Crazy Horse yielded at the Red Cloud Agency in Nebraska on May 6, 1877, not May 5 (p. 105).

Despite these few errors, for its time Victor's book conveyed a large body of important data about then recent events in far-off Wyoming, Montana, and Dakota. Although the time of its appearance dictated a coverage focused more upon causes and campaigns than upon conclusions, as a milestone work of historical literature, *Our Centennial Indian War and the Life of General Custer* stands as the first broadly conceived discourse on the Great Sioux War of 1876–77, with one of the earliest assessments of its foremost military participant. Frances Fuller Victor's work offered order and meaning to a public curious about those events and times, and it assuredly will do so yet today.

Editorial Note

The text of Frances Fuller Victor's Our Centennial Indian War and the Life of General Custer *is reproduced here in its entirety as it was first printed in 1877. Original spellings have been preserved except in the case of obvious typographical errors, which have been corrected. While the content of quotations has not been altered, the punctuation of quotations has been modernized to ensure clarity of presentation.*

Our Centennial Indian War
and the
Life of General Custer

INTRODUCTION

The reader of the foregoing pages can hardly have failed to observe, that the region east of the Big Horn Mountains, including the valleys of the Yellowstone, Big Horn, Powder, and Rosebud Rivers, was the favorite haunt of the Rocky Mountain hunters and trappers—the field of many of their stirring adventures and hardy exploits. Here was the "hunters' paradise," where they came to secure game for food and to feed their animals on the nutritious bark of the cottonwoods; here they assembled at the Summer rendezvous, to exchange their peltries for supplies; and here, oft times, was established their winter camp, with its rough cheer, athletic sports, and wild carousals.

Here, also, between the plains and the mountains, was the dark and sanguinary ground where terrific and deadly combats were fought between the Delawares, Iroquois, Crows, and Blackfeet, and between the trappers and Indians; and here, fifty years later, were enacted scenes of warfare and massacre which cast a gloom over the festivities of our Centennial anniversary.

The recent campaign against the hostile Sioux was over the identical ground where the fur-traders roamed intent on the beaver-skins and adventure; and it is believed that some account thereof, and a sketch of the renowned Indian fighter who perished on the Little Big Horn, may appropriately supplement the story of the Mountain-men.

CHAPTER I

THE SIOUX TRIBES—CAUSES OF THE WAR

THE scene of the campaign against the hostile Indians in 1876, was the rugged, desolate, and partially unexplored region lying between the Big Horn and Powder Rivers, and extending from the Big Horn Mountains northerly to and beyond the Yellowstone River. This region is the most isolated and inaccessible of any lying east of the Rocky Mountains, and is admirably adapted for Indian warfare and defense. Several rivers, tributaries of the Yellowstone, flow through it, and it abounds in creeks, ravines, and canyons. It is the hereditary country of the Crows, who for generations defended it against marauding tribes of Blackfeet.

A vivid description of the general aspect of the country and of the hardships and perils of our soldiers, has been given by Col. Nelson A. Miles, of the Fifth Infantry, in a letter written from the mouth of the Powder River. "No service," he says, "is more thankless or dangerous than contending against these treacherous savages, and if you will come out and learn the real sentiment of the army, you will find the officers of the army

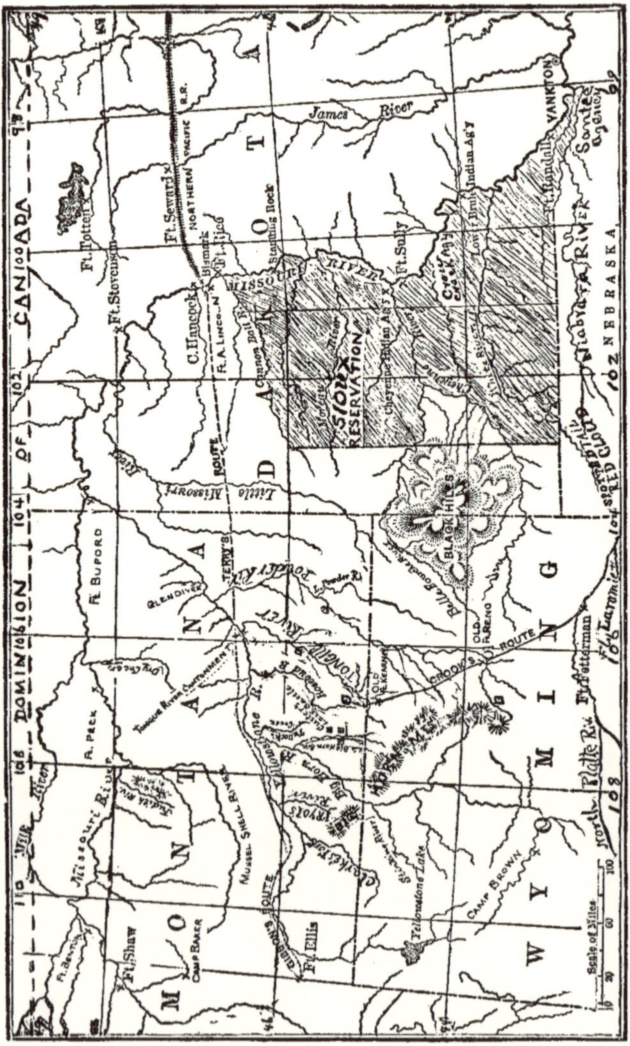

Map of the Sioux country.

the strongest advocates of any peace policy that shall be just and honorable. You will find us out here, five hundred miles from railroad communication, in as barren, desolate and worthless a country as the sun shines upon—volcanic, broken, and almost impassable—so rugged as to make our granite hills of Vermont and New Hampshire appear in comparison as pleasant parks. Jagged and precipitous cliffs; narrow and deep arroyos filled with massive boulders; alkali water, or for miles and miles none at all; and vegetation of cactus and sage-bushes, will represent to you, feebly indeed, the scene of the present campaign, in which we are contending against the most powerful, warlike, and best-armed body of savages on the American Continent, armed and mounted partly at the expense of the Government, and fully supplied with the most improved magazine guns and tons of metallic ammunition."

"The brave mariner," wrote a newspaper correspondent, "on the trackless ocean without compass, is no more at the mercy of wind and wave than Terry's army, out upon this vast trackless waste, is at the mercy of his guides and scouts. The sun rises in the east, shines all day upon a vast expanse of sagebrush and grass, and, as it sets in the west, casts its dull rays into a thousand ravines that neither man nor beast can cross. The magnet always points north; but whether one can go either north or south can be decided only by personal effort. An insignificant turn to the wrong side of a little knoll or buffalo-wallow ofttimes imperceptibly leads the voyager into ravine after ravine, over bluff after bluff, until at last he stands on the edge of a yawning canyon, hundreds of feet in depth and with perpendicular walls. Nothing is left for him to do but to retrace his steps and find an accessible route.

"The hostile Indians with whom our soldiers have had to contend are no despicable foe; on the contrary they are quite able, in frontier warfare, to cope with disciplined troops. They fight in bodies, under skilled leaders, and have regular rules which they observe in battle, on their marches, and in their camps." They have systems of signalling and of scouting, of posting sentinels and videttes, and of herding their animals." They are remarkably expert horsemen, and are so dependent on their steeds, that "a Sioux on foot is a Sioux warrior no longer." Gen. Crook testifies to their adroitness and skill as follows:

> When the Sioux Indian was armed with a bow and arrow he was more formidable, fighting as he does most of the time on horseback, than when he came into possession of the old fashioned muzzle loading rifle. But when he came into possession of the breech loader and metallic cartridge, which allows him to load and fire from his horse with perfect ease, he became at once ten times more formidable. With the improved arms I have seen our friendly Indians, riding at full speed, shoot and kill a wolf, also on the run, while it is a rare thing that our troops can hit an Indian on horseback though the soldier may be on his feet at the time.
>
> The Sioux is a cavalry soldier from the time he has intelligence enough to ride a horse or fire a gun. If he wishes to dismount, his hardy pony, educated by long usage, will graze around near where he has

been left, ready when his master wants to mount either to move forward or escape. Even with their lodges and families they can move at the rate of fifty miles per day. They are perfectly familiar with the country, have their spies and hunting parties out all the time at distances of from twenty to fifty miles each way from their villages, know the number and movements of all the troops that may be operating against them, just about what they can probably do, and hence can choose their own times and places of conflict or avoid it altogether.

The primary causes of the hostilities of the Indians which made this campaign and previous ones against them necessary, extend far back and are too numerous to be here fully stated. The principal Indian grievances however, for which the government is responsible, are a failure to fulfil treaties, encroachment on reserved territories, and the dishonesty of agents. Col. Miles speaks of our relationship with the Indians for the last fifty years, as the dark page in our history, which, next to African slavery, has done more to disgrace our government, blacken our fair name, and reflect upon our civilization, than aught else. It has, he says, been a source of corruption and a disturbing element, unconfined to any one political party or class of individuals.

Wendell Phillips asserts that the worst brutality which prurient malice ever falsely charged the Indian with, is but weak imitation of what the white man has often inflicted on Indian men, women and children; and that the Indian has never lifted his hand against us until provoked to it by misconduct on our part, compared with which, any misconduct of his is but dust in the balance.

The great difference in the condition and character of the Indians over the Canada line and our own, can only be accounted for by the different treatment they have received. The Canadian Indians are, on the whole, a harmless, honest people, who, though they are gradually disappearing before the white man, bear him no ill-will, but rather the contrary. Bishop Whipple of Minnesota, an earnest advocate of the peace policy, draws the following contrast:

> Here are two pictures—on one side of the line a nation has spent $500,000,000 in Indian war; a people who have not 100 miles between the Atlantic and the Pacific which has not been the scene of an Indian massacre; a government which has not passed twenty years without an Indian war; not one Indian tribe to whom it has given Christian civilization; and which celebrates its centennial year by another bloody Indian war. On the other side of the line there is the same greedy, dominant Anglo-Saxon race, and the same heathen. They have not spent one dollar in Indian war; they have had no Indian massacres. Why? In Canada the Indian treaty calls these men "the Indian subjects of her Majesty." When civilization approaches them they are placed on ample reservations; they receive aid in civilization; they have personal rights of property; they are amenable to law and are protected by law; they have schools, and Christian people delight to give them their best men to teach them the religion of Christ. We expend more than one hundred dollars to their one in caring for Indian wards.

The results of the Indian disturbances, whatever their causes, have borne heavily on the hardy and enterprising settlers along the border. Of these citizens Gen. Crook says:

> I believe it is wrong for a Government as great and powerful as ours not to protect its frontier people from savages. I do not see why a man who has the courage to come out here and open the way for civilization in his own country, is not as much entitled to the protection of his Government as anybody else. I am not one of those who believe, as many missionaries sent out here by well-meaning eastern societies do, that the people of the frontiers are cut-throats, thieves, and murderers. I have been thrown among them for nearly 25 years of my life, and believe them to compare favorably in energy, intelligence and manhood with the best of their eastern brethren. They are mercilessly plundered by Indians without any attempt being made to punish the perpetrators, and when they ask for protection, they are told by some of our peace commissioners sent out to make further concessions to the Indians, that they have no business out here anyhow. I do not deny that my sympathies have been with the frontier people in their unequal contest against such obstacles. At the same time I do not wish to be understood as the unrelenting foe of the Indian.

The Sioux Indians, embracing several tribes, are the old Dakotahs, long known as among the bravest and most warlike aboriginals of this continent. They were steadily pushed westward by the tide of civilization to the Great Plains north of the Platte, where they claimed as their own all the vast region west of the Missouri as far as they could roam or fight their way.

They resisted the approach of all settlers and opposed the building of the Pacific Railroad.

In 1867, Congress sent out four civilians and three army officers as Peace Commissioners, who, in 1868, made a treaty with the Sioux, whereby for certain payments or stipulations, they agreed to surrender their claims to a vast tract of country, to live at peace with their neighbors, and to restrict themselves to a territory bounded south by Nebraska, west by the 104th meridian, and north by the 46th parallel of latitude—a territory as large as the State of Michigan. "They had the solemn pledge of the United States that they should be protected in the absolute and peaceable possession of the country thus set apart for them; and the constitution makes such treaties the highest of all authorities, and declares that they are binding upon every citizen."

In the western part of the Sioux territory, lying between the two forks of the Cheyenne River, is the Black Hills country with an area of four or five thousand square miles. Of the interior of this region up to 1874 nothing was known excepting from the indefinite reports of hunters who had penetrated therein. The arrival at a trading post of Indians who offered gold-dust for sale which they said was procured at the Black Hills, caused much excitement; and a military expedition of 1200 men was sent from Fort Lincoln, in July 1874, to explore the Hills and ascertain if gold existed there. As was expected, no hostile enemy were encountered by the large expedition which thus invaded the Indian territory. A few lodges of Indians were met in the Hills, and they ran away notwithstanding friendly overtures were made. An attempt was made to lead the pony of one mounted Indian to headquarters, but he got away, and a shot was fired after him which, says General Custer, wounded either the Indian or his pony as blood was found on the ground.

The geologists of the expedition reported that there was gold in the Black Hills, and miners and others began to flock thither. In 1875, troops were sent to remove the trespassers on the Indian reservation, but as fast as they compelled or persuaded the miners to go away others came to fill their places; and at the present date there are more settlers there than ever before.

Of the treaty of 1868 and the so-called peace policy then inaugurated various opinions are entertained. Gen. Sherman, a member of the commission, in his report for 1876, says:

> The commission had also to treat with other tribes at the south; viz,—the Cheyennes, Arapahoes, Kiowas and Commaches; were engaged for two years in visiting and conferring with these scattered bands; and finally, in 1868, concluded many treaties, which were the best possible at that date, and which resulted in comparative peace on the Plains, by defining clearly the boundaries to be thereafter occupied by the various tribes, with the annuities in money, provisions, and goods to be paid the Indians for the relinquishment of their claims to this vast and indefinite region of land. At this time the Sioux nation consisted of many distinct tribes, and was estimated at 50,000, of whom some 8,000 were named as hostiles.

These Indians, as all others, were under the exclusive jurisdiction of the Indian Bureau, and only small garrisons of soldiers were called for at the several agencies, such as Red Cloud and Spotted Tail on the head of the White Earth River in Nebraska (outside their reservation), and at Standing Rock, Cheyenne, and Crow Creek on the Missouri River, to protect the persons of the agents and their employes. About these several agencies were grouped the several bands of Sioux under various names, receiving food, clothing, etc., and undergoing the process of civilization; but from the time of the Peace Commissson of 1868 to the date of this report, a number of Sioux, recognized as hostile or 'outlaws,' had remained out under the lead of Sitting Bull and a few other chiefs.

"The so-called peace policy," says Bishop Whipple, "was commenced when we were at war. The Indian tribes were either openly hostile, or sullen and turbulent. The new policy was a marvellous success. I do honestly believe that it has done more for the civilization of the Indians than all which the Government has done before. Its only weakness was that the system was not reformed. The new work was fettered by all the faults and traditions of the old policy. The nation left 300,000 men living within our own borders without a vestige of government," without personal rights of property, without the slightest protection of person, property, or life. We persisted in telling these heathen tribes that they were independent nations. We sent out the bravest and best of our officers, some who had grown gray in the service of the country; men whose slightest word was as good as their bond—we sent them because the Indians would not doubt a soldier's honor. They made a treaty, and they pledged the nation's faith that no white man should enter that territory. I do not discuss its wisdom. The Executive and Senate ratified it. . . . A violation of its plain provisions was an act of deliberate perjury. In the words of Gen. Sherman, 'Civilization made its own compact with the weaker party; it was violated, but not by the savage.' The whole world knew that we violated that treaty, and the reason of the failure of the negotiations of last year was that our own commissioners did not have authority from Congress to offer the Indians more than one-third of the sum they were already receiving under the old treaty."

"The Sioux Nation," says Gen. Crook, in his report of Sept. 1876, "numbers many thousands of warriors, and they have been encouraged in their insolent overbearing conduct by the fact, that those who participated in the wholesale massacre of the innocent people in Minnesota during the brief period that preceded their removal to their present location, never received adequate punishment therefor. Following hard upon and as the apparent result of the massacre of over eighty officers and men of the army at Fort Phil Kearney, the Government abandoned three of its military posts, and made a treaty of unparalleled liberality with the perpetrators of these crimes, against whom any other nation would have prosecuted a vigorous war.

"Since that time the reservations, instead of being the abode of loyal Indians holding the terms of their agreement sacred, have been nothing but nests of disloyalty to their treaties and the Government, and scourges to the people whose misfortune it has been to be within the reach of the endurance of their ponies. And in this connection, I regret to say, they have been materially aided by sub-agents who have disgraced a bureau established for the propagation of peace and good will, man to man.

"What is the loyal condition of mind of a lot of savages, who will not allow the folds of the flag of the country to float over the very sugar, coffee and beef, they are kind enough to accept at the hands of the nation to which they have thus far dictated their own terms? Such has been the condition of things at the Red Cloud Agency.

"The hostile bands roamed over a vast extent of country, making the Agencies their base of supplies, their recruiting and ordnance depots, and were so closely connected by intermarriage, interest and common cause with the Agency Indians, that it was difficult to determine where the line of peaceably disposed ceased and the hostile commenced. They have, without interruption, attacked persons at home, murdered and scalped them, stolen their stock—in fact violated every leading feature in the treaty. Indeed, so great were their depredations on the stock belonging to the settlers, that at certain times they have not had sufficient horses to do their ordinary farming work—all the horses being concentrated on the Sioux Reservation or among the bands which owe allegiance to what is called the Sioux Nation. In the winter months these renegade bands dwindle down to a comparatively small number; while in summer they are recruited by restless spirits from the different reservations, attracted by the opportunity to plunder the frontiersman, so that by midsummer they become augmented from small bands of one hundred to thousands.

"In fact, it was well known that the treaty of 1868 had been regarded by the Indians as an instrument binding on us but not binding on them. On the part of the Government, notwithstanding the utter disregard by the Sioux of the terms of the treaty, stringent orders, enforced by military power, had been issued prohibiting settlers from trespassing upon the country known as the Black Hills. The people of the country against whom the provisions of the treaty were so rigidly enforced naturally complained that if they were required to observe this treaty, some effort should be made to compel the Indians to observe it likewise.

"The occupation by the settlers of the Black Hills country had nothing to do with the hostilities which have been in progress. In fact, by the continuous violations by these Indians of the treaty referred to, the settlers were furnished with at least a reasonable excuse for such occupation, in that a treaty so long and persistently violated by the Indians themselves, should not be quoted as a valid instrument for the preventing of such occupation. Since the occupation of the Black Hills there has not been any greater number of depredations committed by the Indians than previous to such occupation; in truth, the people who have gone to the Hills have not suffered any more and probably not as much from Indians, as they would had they remained at their homes along the border."

"In 1868," says Wm. R. Steele, delegate from Wyoming, "the United States made a treaty with the Sioux Nation, which was a grave mistake, if it was not a national dishonor and disgrace; that treaty has been the foundation of all the difficulties in the Sioux country. In 1866, Gen. Pope established posts at Fort Phil Kearney, Reno, and Fort Smith, so as to open the road to Montana and protect the country and friendly Crows from the hostile Sioux. In keeping these posts and opening that road, many men, citizens and soldiers, had been killed. Notable among the actions that had taken place was the massacre of Fetterman and his command at Fort Phil Kearney; and yet after these men had sacrificed their lives, the Government went to work and made a treaty by which it ignominiously abandoned that country to these savages, dismantling its own forts, and leaving there the bones of men who had laid down their lives in the wilderness. Was it to be wondered at, under these circumstances, that Sitting Bull and his men believed they were superior to the general government? Any body who knows anything about Indian nature knows that the legitimate result of that cowardly policy of peace at any price, was to defer only the evil day which has now come upon us. Since that time the Sioux have been constantly depredating on the frontiers of Nebraska, Wyoming and Montana, and more men have fallen there in the peaceful vocations of civil life, without a murmur being heard, than fell under the gallant Custer. The friendly Crows have been raided with every full moon; so with the Shoshones; and at last these outrages have become so great and so long continued that even the peaceable Indian Department could not stand them any longer, and called on the military arm of the Government to punish these men."

President Grant, in his message of December, 1876, uses the following language: "A policy has been adopted towards the Indian tribes inhabiting a large portion of the territory of the United States, which has been humane, and has substantially ended Indian hostilities in the whole land, except in a portion of Nebraska, and Dakota, Wyoming, and Montana territories, the Black Hills region, and approaches thereto. Hostilities there have grown out of the avarice of the white man, who has violated our treaty stipulations in his search for gold. The question might be asked, why the Government had not enforced obedience to the terms of the treaty prohibiting the occupation of the Black Hills region by whites? The answer is simple. The first immigrants to the Black Hills were removed by troops, but rumors of rich discoveries of gold took into that region increased numbers. Gold has actually been found in paying quantity, and an effort to remove the miners would only result in the desertion of the bulk of the troops that might be sent there to remove them."

The causes and objects of the military operations against the Sioux in 1876, as stated by the Secretary of War in a letter to the President dated July 8th, 1876, were in part as follows:

The present military operations are not against the Sioux nation at all, but against certain hostile parts of it which defy the Government, and are undertaken at the special request of the bureau of the Government charged with their supervision, and wholly to make the civilization of the remainder possible. No part of these operations are on or near the Sioux reservation. The accidental discovery of gold on the western border of the Sioux reservation and the intrusion of our people thereon have not caused this war, and have only complicated it by the uncertainty of numbers to be encountered. The young warriors love war, and frequently escape their agents to go to the hunt or war path—their only idea of the object of life. The object of these military expeditions was in the interest of the peaceful parts of the Sioux nation, supposed to embrace at least nine-tenths of the whole, and not one of these peaceful treaty Indians has been molested by the military authorities.

Of the hostile Indians referred to by the Secretary of War, Hon. E. P. Smith, Commissioner of Indian Affairs, reported Nov. 1st, 1875: "It will probably be found necessary to compel the Northern non-treaty Sioux, under the leadership of Sitting Bull, who have never yet in any way recognized the United States Government, except by snatching rations occasionally at an agency, and such outlaws from the several agencies as have attached themselves to these same hostiles, to cease marauding and settle down, as the other Sioux have done, at some designated point."

Soon afterwards, Indian Inspector E. C. Watkins addressed the Commissioner respecting these Indians, as follows: "The true policy in my judgment is to send troops against them in winter, the sooner the better, and whip them into subjection. They richly merit punishment for their incessant warfare and their numerous murders of white settlers and their families, or white men whenever found unarmed."

Early in December, by the advice of the Secretary of the Interior, Commissioner Smith directed that runners be sent out to notify "said Indian Sitting Bull, and others outside their reservation, that they must move to the reservation before the 31st day of January, 1876; that if they neglect or refuse so to move, they will be reported to the War Department as hostile Indians, and that a military force will be sent to compel them to obey the order of the Indian officer." Respecting this order to the Indians, Bishop Whipple, in a letter to the *New York Tribune*, says:

> There was an inadequate supply of provisions at the agencies that Fall, and the Indians went out to their unceded territory to hunt. They went as they were accustomed to do—with the consent of their agents and as provided by the treaty. * * * The Indians had gone away from the agencies to secure food, and skins for clothing. The United States had set apart this very country as a hunting-ground for them forever. Eight months after this order to return or be treated as hostile, Congress appropriated money for the seventh of thirty installments for these roaming Indians. It was impossible for the Indians to obey the order. No one of the runners sent out to inform the Indians, was able to return himself by the time appointed; yet Indian women and children were expected to travel a treeless desert, without food or proper clothing, under the penalty of death.

As the order and warning were disregarded by the Indians, the Secretary of the Interior notified the Secretary of War, Feb. 1st, 1876, that "the time given him (Sitting Bull) in which to return to an agency having expired, and advices received at the Indian Office being to the effect that Sitting Bull still refuses to comply with the direction of the Commissioner, the said Indians are hereby turned over to the War Department for such action on the part of the army as you may deem proper under the circumstances."

By direction of Lieut. General Sheridan, Commander over the vast extent of territory included in the Military Division of Missouri, Brig. Gen. George Crook, Commander of the Department of the Platte, an officer of great merit and experience in Indian fighting, now undertook to reduce these Indian outlaws to subjection, and made preparations for an expedition against them.

CHAPTER II

BATTLES OF THE POWDER AND ROSEBUD

General Crook started from Fort Fetterman, W. T., March 1st, 1876, at the head of an expedition composed of ten companies of the 2d and 3d Cavalry under Col. J. J. Reynolds, and two companies of the 4th Infantry, with teamsters, guides, etc., amounting in all to nearly nine hundred men. His course was nearly north, past the abandoned Forts Reno and Phil. Kearney to Tongue River. He descended this river nearly to the Yellowstone, scouted Rosebud River, and then changed his course to the south-east toward Powder River. At a point on the head of Otter Creek, Crook divided his command, and sent Col. Reynolds with six companies of cavalry and one day's rations to follow the trail of two Indians discovered that day in the snow.

Col. Reynolds moved at 5 P.M. of the 16th, and at 4.20 A.M., after a night's march of thirty miles, was near the forks of Powder River. The following extracts are copied from a letter written to the *New York Tribune*:

> A halt was called here and the column took shelter in a ravine. No fires were allowed to be kindled, nor even a match lighted. The cold

was intense and seemed to be at least 30° below zero. The command remained here till about 6 o'clock, doing their uttermost to keep from freezing, the scouts meantime going out to reconnoitre. At this hour they returned, reporting a larger and fresher trail leading down to the river which was about four miles distant. The column immediately started on the trail. The approach to the river seemed almost impracticable. Before reaching the final precipices which overlooked the riverbed, the scouts discovered that a village lay in the valley at the foot of the bluffs. It was now 8 o'clock. The sun shone brightly through the cold frosty air.

The column halted, and Noyes's battalion, 2d Cavalry, was ordered up to the front. It consisted of Company I, Capt. Noyes, and Company K, Capt. Egan. This battalion was ordered to descend to the valley, and while Egan charged the camp, Noyes was to cut out the herd of horses feeding close by and drive it up the river. Capt. Moore's battalion of two companies was ordered to dismount and proceed along the edge of the ridge to a position covering the eastern side of the village opposite that from which Egan was to charge. Capt. Mills's battalion was ordered to follow Egan dismounted, and support him in the engagement which might follow the charge.

These columns began the descent of the mountain, through gorges which were almost perpendicular. Nearly two hours were occupied in getting the horses of the charging columns down these rough sides of the mountain, and even then, when a point was reached where the men could mount their horses and proceed toward the village in the narrow valley beneath, Moore's battalion had not been able to gain its position on the eastern side after clambering along the edges of the mountain. A few Indians could be seen with the herd, driving it to the edge of the river, but nothing indicated that they knew of our approach.

Just at 9 o'clock Capt. Egan turned the point of the mountain nearest the river, and first in a walk and then in a rapid trot started for the village. The company went first in column of twos, but when within 200 yards of the village the command "Left front into line" was given, and with a yell they rushed into the encampment. Capt. Noyes had in the meantime wheeled to the right and started the herd up the river. With the yell of the charging column the Indians sprang up as if by magic and poured in a rapid fire from all sides. Egan charged through and through the village before Moore's and Mills's battalions got within supporting distance, and finding things getting very hot, formed his line in some high willows on the south side of the camp, from which he poured in rapid volleys upon the Indians.

Up to this time the Indians supposed that one company was all they had to contend with, but when the other battalions appeared, rapidly advancing, deployed as skirmishers and pouring in a galling fire of musketry, they broke on all sides and took refuge in the rocks along the side of the mountain. The camp, consisting of 110 lodges, with immense quantities of robes, fresh meat, and plunder of all kinds, with over 700 head of horses were in our possession. The work of burning immediately began, and soon the whole encampment was in flames.

After the work of destruction was completed the whole command moved rapidly up the river twenty miles to Lodgepole Creek. This point was reached at nightfall by all except Moore's battalion and Egan's company. Company E was the rear guard, and assisted Major Stanton and the scouts in bringing up the herd of horses; many of these were shot on the road, and the remainder reached camp about 9 P.M. These troops had been in the saddle for 36 hours, with the exception of five hours during which they were fighting, and all, officers and men, were much exhausted.

Upon arriving at Lodgepole, it was found that General Crook and the other four companies and pack-train had not arrived, so that everybody was supperless and without a blanket. The night, therefore, was not a cheerful one, but not a murmur was heard. The tired men lay upon the snow or leaned against a tree, and slept as best they could on so cold a night. Saturday, at noon, General Crook arrived. In the meantime a portion of the herd of horses had straggled into the ravines, and fallen into the hands of the Indians.

The village thus destroyed was that of Crazy Horse, one of the avowedly hostile chiefs. "He had with him," wrote Gen. Crook, "the Northern Cheyennes, and some of the Minneconjous—probably in all one-half of the Indians off the reservations." The Indian loss was unknown. Four of Reynolds' men were killed, and six men including one officer were wounded. The whole force subsequently returned to Fort Fetterman, reaching there March 26th.

The results of this expedition were neither conclusive or satisfactory. Therefore, Gen. Sheridan determined to proceed more systematically by concentric movements. He ordered three distinct columns to be prepared to move to a common centre, where the hostiles were supposed to be, from Montana, from Dakota, and from the Platte. The two former fell under the command of Gen. Alfred H. Terry, Commander of the Department of Dakota, and the latter under Gen. Crook. These movements were to be simultaneous, so that Indians avoiding one column might be encountered by another.

Gen. Crook marched from Fort Fetterman on the 29th of May, with two battalions of the 2d and 3d Cavalry under Lieut. Col. W. B. Royall, and a battalion of five companies of the 4th and 9th Infantry under Major Alex. Chambers, with a train of wagons, pack-mules, and Indian scouts, all amounting to 47 officers and 1,000 men present for duty. This expedition marched by the same route as the preceding one, to a point on Goose Creek, which is the head of Tongue River, where a supply camp was established on June 8th. During the preceding night a party of Sioux came down on the encampment, and endeavored to stampede the horses, bringing on an engagement which resulted in the discomfiture and retreat of the enemy. On the 14th, a band of Shoshones and Crows—Indians unfriendly to the Sioux—joined Crook, and were provided with arms and ammunition.

The aggressive column of the expedition resumed the march forward on the morning of the 16th, leaving the trains parked at the Goose Creek camp. The infantry were mounted on mules borrowed from the pack-train, and each man carried his own supplies consisting of only three days' rations and one blanket. At night, after marching about 35 miles, the little army encamped between high bluffs at the head waters of Rosebud River.

At 5 A.M. on the morning of the 17th the troops started down the valley of the Rosebud, the Indian allies marching in front and on the flanks. After advancing about seven miles successive shots were heard in front, the scouts came running in to report Indians advancing, and Gen. Crook had hardly time to form his men, before large numbers of warriors fully prepared for a fight were in view.

The battle which ensued was on both banks of the Rosebud, near the upper end of a deep canyon having sides which were steep, covered with pine, and apparently impregnable, through which the stream ran. The Indians displayed a strong force at all points, and contested the ground with a tenacity which indicated that they were fighting for time to remove their village, which was supposed to be about six miles down the Rosebud at the lower end of the canyon, or believed themselves strong enough to defeat their opponents.

The officers and men of Crook's command behaved with marked gallantry during the engagement. The Sioux were finally repulsed in their bold onset, and lost many of their bravest warriors; but when they fled they could not be pursued far without great danger owing to the roughness of the country. The Indian allies were full of enthusiasm but not very manageable, preferring to fight independently of orders. Crook's losses were nine soldiers killed, and twenty-one wounded, including Capt. Henry of the 3d Cavalry. Seven of the friendly Indians were wounded, and one was killed.

Gen. Crook was satisfied that the number and quality of the enemy required more men than he had, and being encumbered with wounded he concluded to retreat. The night was passed on the battle-field, and the next day he started for his camp on Goose Creek, which was reached June 19th. Couriers were sent to Fort Fetterman for reinforcements and supplies, and the command remained inactive for several weeks awaiting their arrival.

The battle of the Rosebud was fought not very far from the scene of Custer's defeat a few days later, and Gen. Crook concludes that his opponents were the same that Custer and Reno encountered.

"It now became apparent," says Gen. Sheridan in his report "that Gen. Crook had not only Crazy Horse and his small band to contend with, but that the hostile force had been augmented by large numbers of the young warriors from the agencies along the Missouri River, and the Red Cloud and Spotted Tail agencies in Nebraska, and that the Indian agents at these agencies had concealed the fact of the departure of these warriors, and that in most cases they continued to issue rations as though they were present."

CHAPTER III

TERRY'S EXPEDITION—OPENING OF THE CAMPAIGN

General Terry left Fort Abraham Lincoln on the Missouri River, May 17th 1876, with his division, consisting of the 7th Cavalry under Lieut. Col. George A. Custer, three companies of infantry, a battery of Gatling guns, and 45 enlisted scouts. His whole force, exclusive of the wagon-train drivers, numbered about 1000 men. His march was westerly, over the route taken by the Stanley expedition in 1873.

On the 11th of June, Terry reached the south bank of the Yellowstone at the mouth of Powder River, where by appointment he met steamboats, and established his supply camp. A scouting party of six companies of the 7th Cavalry under Major M. A. Reno was sent out June 10th, which ascended Powder River to its forks, crossed westerly to Tongue River and beyond, and discovered, near Rosebud River, a heavy Indian trail about ten days old leading westward toward Little Big Horn River. After following this trail a short distance Reno returned to the Yellowstone and rejoined his regiment, which then marched, accompanied by steamboats, to the mouth of Rosebud River where it encamped June 21st. Communication by steamboats and scouts had previously been opened with Col. John Gibbon, whose column was at this time encamped on the north side of the Yellowstone, near by.

Col. Gibbon of the 7th Infantry had left Fort Ellis in Montana about the middle of May, with a force consisting of six companies of his regiment, and four companies of the 2d Cavalry under Major J. S. Brisbin. He had marched eastward down the north bank of the Yellowstone to the mouth of the Rosebud, where he encamped about June 1st.

Gen. Terry now consulted with Gibbon and Custer, and decided upon a plan for attacking the Indians who were believed to be assembled in large numbers near [Little] Big Horn River. Custer with his regiment was to ascend the valley of the Rosebud, and then turn towards Little Big Horn River, keeping well to the south. Gibbon's troops were to cross the Yellowstone at the mouth of Big Horn River, and march up the Big Horn to its junction with the Little Big Horn, to co-operate with Custer. It was hoped that the Indians would thus be brought between the two forces so that their escape would be impossible.

Col. Gibbon's column was immediately put in motion for the mouth of the Big Horn. On the next day, June 22d, at noon, Custer announced himself ready to start, and drew out his regiment. It consisted of 12 companies, numbering 28 officers and 747 soldiers. There were also a strong detachment of scouts and guides, several civilians, and a supply train of 185 pack mules. Gen. Terry reviewed the column in the presence of Gibbon and Brisbin, and it was pronounced in splendid condition. "The officers clustered around Terry for a final shake of the hand, the last good-bye was said, and in the best of spirits, filled with high hopes, they galloped away—many of them to their death."

Gen. Terry's orders to Custer were as follows:

CAMP AT THE MOUTH OF THE ROSEBUD RIVER,
June 22d, 1876.

Lieut. Col. Custer, 7th Cavalry.

COLONEL: The Brigadier General Commanding directs that as soon as your regiment can be made ready for the march, you proceed up the Rosebud in pursuit of the Indians whose trail was discovered by Major Reno a few days ago. It is, of course, impossible to give any definite instructions in regard to this movement, and, were it not impossible to do so, the Department Commander places too much confidence in your zeal, energy, and ability to wish to impose upon you precise orders which might hamper your action when nearly in contact with the enemy. He will, however, indicate to you his own views of what your action should be, and he desires that you should conform to them unless you shall see sufficient reason for departing from them. He thinks that you should proceed up the Rosebud until you ascertain definitely the direction in which the trail above spoken of leads. Should it be found (as it appears to be almost certain that it will be found) to turn towards the Little Big Horn, he thinks that you should still proceed southward perhaps as far as the head waters of the Tongue, and then turn toward the Little Big Horn, feeling constantly, however, to your left, so as to preclude the possibility of the escape of the Indians to the south or south-east by passing around your left flank. The column of Col. Gibbon is now in motion for the mouth of the Big Horn. As soon as it reaches that point it will cross the Yellowstone, and move up at least as far as the forks of the Big and Little Big Horn. Of course its future movements must be controlled by circumstances as they arise; but it is hoped that the Indians, if up on the Little Big Horn, may be so nearly inclosed by the two columns that their escape will be impossible. The Department Commander desires that on your way up the Rosebud you should thoroughly examine the upper part of Tulloch's Creek, and that you should endeavor to send a scout through to Col. Gibbon's column with information of the result of your examination. The lower part of this creek will be examined by a detachment from Col. Gibbon's command. The supply steamer will be pushed up the Big Horn as far as the forks of the river are found to be navigable for that space, and the Department Commander, who will accompany the column of Col. Gibbon, desires you to report to him there not later than the expiration of the time for which your troops are rationed, unless in the meantime you receive further orders. Respectfully &c.,

E. W. Smith, Captain 18th Infantry,
Acting Assistant Adjutant General.

After proceeding southerly up the Rosebud for about seventy miles, Custer, at 11 P.M. on the night of the 24th, turned westerly towards Little Big Horn River. The next morning while crossing the elevated land between the two rivers, a large Indian village was discovered about fifteen miles distant, just across Little Big Horn River. Custer with characteristic promptness decided to attack the village at once.

One company was escorting the train at the rear. The balance of the force was divided into three columns. The trail they were on led down to the stream at a point some distance south of the village. Major Reno, with three companies under Capt. T. H. French, Capt. Myles Moylan, and Lieut. Donald McIntosh, was ordered to follow the trail, cross the stream, and charge down its north bank. Capt. F. W. Benteen, with his own company and two others under Capt. T. B. Weir and Lieut. E. S. Godfrey, was sent to make a detour to the south of Reno. The other five companies of the regiment, under the immediate command of Custer, formed the right of the little army.

On reaching the river Reno crossed it as ordered, and Custer with his five companies turned northerly into a ravine running behind the bluffs on the east side of the stream.

CHAPTER IV

GIBBON'S MARCH UP THE BIG HORN RIVER

THE supply steamer Far West with Gen. Terry and Col. Gibbon on board, which steamed up the Yellowstone on the evening of June 23d, overtook Gibbon's troops near the mouth of the Big Horn early on the morning of the 24th; and by 4 o'clock P.M. of the same day, the entire command with the animals and supplies had been ferried over to the south side of the Yellowstone. An hour later the column marched out to and across Tulloch's Creek, and then encamped for the night.

At 5 o'clock on the morning of the 25th, (Sunday) the column was again in motion; and after marching 22 miles over a country so rugged as to task the endurance of the men to the utmost, the infantry halted for the night. Gen. Terry, however, with the cavalry and the battery pushed on 14 miles further in hopes of opening communication with Custer, and camped at midnight near the mouth of the Little Big Horn.

Scouts sent out from Terry's camp early on the morning of the 26th discovered three Indians, who proved to be Crows who had accompanied Custer's regiment. They reported that a battle had been fought and that the Indians were killing white men in great numbers. Their story was not fully credited, as it was not expected that a conflict would occur so soon, or believed that serious disaster could have overtaken so large a force.

The infantry, which had broken camp very early, now came up, and the whole column crossed the Little Big Horn and moved up its western valley. It was soon reported that a dense heavy smoke was resting over the southern horizon far ahead, and in a short time it became visible to all. This was hailed as a sign that Custer had met the Indians, defeated them, and burned their village. The weary foot soldiers were elated and freshened by the sight, and pressed on with increased spirit and speed.

Custer's position was believed to be not far ahead, and efforts were repeatedly made during the afternoon to open communication with him; but the scouts who attempted to go through were met and driven back by hostile Indians who were hovering in the front. As evening came on, their numbers increased and large parties could be seen on the bluffs hurrying from place to place and watching every movement of the advancing soldiers.

At 8:40 in the evening the infantry had marched that day about 30 miles. The forks of the Big Horn, the place where Terry had requested Custer to report to him, were many miles behind and the expected messenger from Custer had not arrived. Daylight was fading, the men were fatigued, and the column was therefore halted for the night. The animals were picketed, guards were set, and the weary men, wrapped in their blankets and with their weapons beside them, were soon asleep on the ground.

Early on the morning of the 27th the march up the Little Big Horn was resumed. The smoke cloud was still visible and apparently but a short distance ahead. Soon a dense grove of trees was reached and passed through cautiously, and then the head of the column entered a beautiful level meadow about a mile in width, extending along the west side of the stream and overshadowed east and west by high bluffs. It soon became apparent that this meadow had recently been the site of an immense Indian village, and the great number of temporary brushwood and willow huts indicated that many Indians beside the usual inhabitants had rendezvoused there. It was also evident that it had been hastily deserted. Hundreds of lodge-poles, with finely-dressed buffalo-robes and other hides, dried meat, stores, axes, utensils, and Indian trinkets were left behind; and in two tepees or lodges still standing, were the bodies of nine Indians who had gone to the "happy hunting-grounds."

Every step of the march now revealed some evidence that a conflict had taken place not far away. The dead bodies of Indian horses were seen, and cavalry equipments and weapons, bullet-pierced clothing, and blood-stained gloves were picked up; and at last the bodies of soldiers and their horses gave positive proof that a disastrous battle had taken place. The Crow Indians had told the truth.

The head of the column was now met by a breathless scout, who came running up with the intelligence that Major Reno with a body of troops was intrenched on a bluff further on, awaiting relief. The soldiers pushed ahead in the direction pointed out, and soon came in sight of men and horses intrenched on top of a hill on the opposite or east side of the river. Terry and Gibbon immediately forded the stream and rode toward the group. As they approached the top of the hill, they were welcomed by hearty cheers from a swarm of soldiers who came out of their intrenchments to meet their deliverers. The scene was a touching one. Stout-hearted soldiers who had kept bravely up during the hours of conflict and danger now cried like children, and the pale faces of the wounded lighted up as hope revived within them.

The story of the relieved men briefly told was as follows: After separating from Custer about noon, June 25th, (as related in the last chapter) Reno proceeded to the river, forded it, and charged down its west bank toward the village, meeting at first with but little resistance. Soon however he was attacked by such numbers as to be obliged to dismount his men, shelter his horses in a strip of woods, and fight on foot. Finding that they would soon be surrounded and defeated, he again mounted his men, and charging upon such of the enemy as obstructed his way, retreated across the river, and reached the top of a bluff followed closely by Indians. Just then Benteen, returning from his detour southward, discovered Reno's perilous position, drove back the Indians, and joined him on the hill. Shortly afterward, the company which was escorting the mule train also joined Reno. The seven companies thus brought together had been subsequently assailed by Indians; many of the men had been killed and wounded, and it was only by obstinate resistance that they had been enabled to defend themselves in an entrenched position. The enemy had retired on the evening of the 26th.

After congratulations to Reno and his brave men for their successful defence enquiries were made respecting Custer, but no one could tell where he was. Neither he or any of his men had been seen since the fight commenced, and the musketry heard from the direction he took had ceased on the afternoon of the 25th. It was supposed by Reno and Benteen that he had been repulsed, and retreated northerly towards Terry's troops.

A search for Custer and his men was immediately begun, and it revealed a scene calculated to appall the stoutest heart. Although neither Custer nor any of that part of his regiment which he led to combat were found alive to tell the tale, an examination of their trail and the scene of conflict enabled their comrades to form some idea of the engagement in which they perished.

CHAPTER V

CUSTER'S LAST BATTLE

GENERAL CUSTER's trail, from the place where he left Reno's and turned northward, passed along and in the rear of the crest of hills on the east bank of the stream for nearly three miles, and then led, through an opening in the bluff, down to the river. Here Custer had evidently attempted to cross over to attack the village. The trail then turned back on itself, as if Custer had been repulsed and obliged to retreat, and branched to the northward, as if he had been prevented from returning southerly by the way he came, or had determined to retreat in the direction from which Terry's troops were advancing.

Several theories as to the subsequent movements of the troops have been entertained by persons who visited the grounds. One is, that the soldiers in retreating took advantage of two ravines; that two companies under Capt. T. W. Custer and Lieut. A. E. Smith, were led by Gen. Custer up the ravine nearest the river, while the upper ravine furnished a line of retreat for the three companies of Capt. G. W. Yates, Capt. M. W. Keogh, and Lieut. James Calhoun. At the head of this upper ravine, a mile from the river, a stand had been made by Calhoun's company; the skirmish lines were marked by rows of the slain with heaps of empty cartridge shells before them, and Lieuts. Calhoun and Crittenden lay dead just behind the files. Further on, Capt. Keogh had fallen surrounded by his men; and still further on, upon a hill, Capt. Yates' company took its final stand. Here, according to this theory, Yates was joined by what remained of the other two companies, who had been furiously assailed in the lower ravine; and here Gen. Custer and the last survivors of the five companies met their death, fighting bravely to the end.

Another theory of the engagement is, that Custer attempted to retreat up the lower ravine in columns of companies; that the companies of Custer and Smith being first in the advance and last in the retreat, fell first in the slaughter which followed the retrograde movement; that Yates' company took the position on the hill, and perished there with Custer and other officers; and that the two other companies, Keogh's and Calhoun's, perished while fighting their way back towards Reno—a few reaching the place where Custer first struck the high banks of the river.

Still another theory is, that the main line of retreat was by the upper ravine; that Calhoun's company was thrown across to check the Indians, and was the first annihilated. That the two companies of Capt. Custer and Lieut. Smith retreated from the place where Gen. Custer was killed into the lower ravine, and were the last survivors of the conflict.

Near the highest point of the hill lay the body of General Custer, and near by were those of his brother Captain Custer, Lieut. Smith, Capt. Yates, Lieut. W. V. Riley of Yates' company, and Lieut. W. W. Cooke. Some distance away, close together, were found another brother of Gen. Custer—Boston Custer, a civilian, who had accompanied the expedition as forage master of the 7th Cavalry—and his nephew Armstrong Reed, a youth of nineteen, who was visiting the General at the time the expedition started, and accompanied it as a driver of the herd of cattle taken along. The wife of Lieut. Calhoun was a sister of the Custer's, and she here lost her husband, three brothers, and a nephew.

Other officers of Custer's battalion killed but not already mentioned, were Asst. Surgeon L. W. Lord, and Lieuts. H. M. Harrington, J. E. Porter, and J. G. Sturgis. The last named was a West Point graduate of 1875, and a son of General S. D. Sturgis, the Colonel of the 7th Cavalry, who had been detained by other duties when his regiment started on this expedition. The bodies of the slain were rifled of valuables and all were mutilated excepting Gen. Custer, and Mark Kellogg—a correspondent of the *New York Herald*. Gen. Custer was clad in a buckskin suit; and a Canadian—Mr. Macdonald—was subsequently informed by Indians who were in the fight, that for this reason he was not mangled, as they took him to be some brave hunter accidentally with the troops. Others believe that Custer was passed by from respect for the heroism of one whom the Indians had learned to fear and admire.

The dead were buried June 28th, where they fell, Major Reno and the survivors of his regiment performing the last sad rites over their comrades.

A retreat to the mouth of Big Horn River was now ordered and successfully effected, the wounded being comfortably transported on mule litters to the mouth of the Little Big Horn, where they were placed on a steamboat and taken to Fort Lincoln. Gibbon's Cavalry followed the Indians for about ten miles, and ascertained that they had moved to the south and west by several trails. A good deal of property had been thrown away by them to lighten their march, and was found scattered about. Many of their dead were also discovered secreted in ravines a long distance from the battle field.

At the boat was found one of Custer's scouts, who had been in the fight—a Crow named Curley; his story was as follows:

> Custer kept down the river on the north bank four miles, after Reno had crossed to the south side above. He thought Reno would drive down the valley, to attack the village at the upper end, while he (Custer) would go in at the lower end. Custer had to go further down the river and further away from Reno than he wished on account of the steep bank along the north side; but at last he found a ford and dashed for it. The Indians met him and poured in a heavy fire from across the narrow river. Custer dismounted to fight on foot, but could not get his skirmishers over the stream. Meantime hundreds of Indians, on foot and

on ponies, poured over the river, which was only about three feet deep, and filled the ravine on each side of Custer's men. Custer then fell back to some high ground behind him and seized the ravines in his immediate vicinity. The Indians completely surrounded Custer and poured in a terrible fire on all sides. They charged Custer on foot in vast numbers, but were again and again driven back.

The fight began about 2 o'clock, and lasted almost until the sun went down over the hills. The men fought desperately, and after the ammunition in their belts was exhausted went to their saddlebags, got more and continued the fight. Custer lived until nearly all his men had been killed or wounded, and went about encouraging his soldiers to fight on. He got a shot in the left side and sat down, with his pistol in his hand. Another shot struck Custer in the breast, and he fell over. The last officer killed was a man who rode a white horse—believed to be Lieut. Cooke, as Cooke and Calhoun were the only officers who rode white horses.

When he [Curley] saw Custer hopelessly surrounded he watched his opportunity, got a Sioux blanket, put it on, and worked up a ravine, and when the Sioux charged, he got among them and they did not know him from one of their own men. There were some mounted Sioux, and seeing one fall, he ran to him, mounted his pony, and galloped down as if going towards the white men, but went up a ravine and got away. As he rode off he saw, when nearly a mile from the battle field, a dozen or more soldiers in a ravine, fighting with Sioux all around them. He thinks all were killed, as they were outnumbered five to one, and apparently dismounted. The battle was desperate in the extreme, and more Indians than white men must have been killed.

The following extract is from a letter written to Gen. Sheridan by Gen. Terry at his camp on the Big Horn, July 2d:

We calculated it would take Gibbon's command until the 26th to reach the mouth of the Little Big Horn, and that the wide sweep I had proposed Custer should make would require so much time that Gibbon would be able to co-operate with him in attacking any Indians that might be found on the stream. I asked Custer how long his marches would be. He said they would be at the rate of about 30 miles a day. Measurements were made and calculations based on that rate of progress. I talked with him about his strength, and at one time suggested that perhaps it would be well for me to take Gibbon's cavalry and go with him. To the latter suggestion he replied: that, without reference to the command, he would prefer his own regiment alone. As a homogeneous body, as much could be done with it as with the two combined. He expressed the utmost confidence that he had all the force that he could need, and I shared his confidence. The plan adopted was the only one which promised to bring the infantry into action, and I desired to make sure of things by getting up every available man. I offered Custer the battery of Gatling guns, but he declined it, saying that it might embarrass him, and that he was strong enough without it. The movements proposed by General Gibbon's column were carried out to the letter, and had the attack been deferred until it was up, I cannot doubt that we should have been successful.

CHAPTER VI

RENO'S BATTLES ON THE LITTLE BIG HORN

AFTER the battle in which Lieut. Col. Custer lost his life, the command of the 7th Cavalry regiment devolved on Major Reno. The following is a copy of Reno's official report to Gen. Terry, excepting that a few unimportant paragraphs are omitted. It is dated July 5th, 1876.

The regiment left the camp at the mouth of Rosebud River, after passing in review before the department commander, under command of Brevet Major General G. A. Custer, Lieutenant Colonel, on the afternoon of the 22d of June, and marched up the Rosebud 12 miles and encamped. 23d—Marched up the Rosebud, passing many old Indian camps, and following a very large lodge-pole trail, but not fresh, making 33 miles. 24th—The march was continued up the Rosebud, the trail and signs freshening with every mile until we had made 28 miles, and we then encamped and waited for information from the scouts. At 9.25 P.M., Custer called the officers together, and informed us that beyond a doubt the village was in the valley of the Little Big Horn, and that to reach it, it was necessary to cross the divide between the Rosebud and Little Big Horn, and it would be impossible to do so in the daytime without discovering our march to the Indians; that we would prepare to move at 11 P.M. This was done, the line of march turning from the Rosebud to the right, up one of its branches, which headed near the summit of the divide.

About 2 A.M. of the 25th, the scouts told him that he could not cross the divide before daylight. We then made coffee and rested for three hours, at the expiration of which time the march was resumed, the divide crossed, and about 8 A.M. the command was in the valley of one of the branches of the Little Big Horn. By this time Indians had been seen, and it was certain that we could not surprise them, and it was determined to move at once to the attack.

Previous to this no division of the regiment had been made since the order was issued on the Yellowstone, annulling wing and battalion organizations. General Custer informed me he would assign commands on the march. I was ordered by Lieut. W. W. Cooke, Adjutant, to assume command of Companies M, A, and G; Capt. Benteen of Companies H, D, and K; Custer retaining C, E, F, I, and L, under his immediate command; and Company B, Capt. McDougall, being in rear of the pack train. I assumed command of the companies assigned to me, and without any definite orders, moved forward with the rest of the column, and well to its left. I saw Benteen moving further to the left, and, as they passed, he told me he had orders to move well to the left, and sweep everything before him; I did not see him again until about 2:30 P.M. The command moved down the creek towards the Little Big Horn Valley. Custer with five companies on the right bank; myself and three companies on the left bank; and Benteen further to the left, and out of sight.

As we approached a deserted village, in which was standing one tepee, about 11 A.M., Custer motioned me to cross to him, which I did, and moved nearer to his column, until about 12:30 A.M., when Lieut. Cooke came to me and said the village was only two miles ahead and running away. To "move forward at as rapid a gait as I thought prudent and to charge afterward, and that the whole outfit would support me." I think those were his exact words. I at once took a fast trot, and moved down about two miles, when I came to a ford of the river. I crossed immediately, and halted about ten minutes or less, to gather the battalion, sending word to Custer that I had everything in front of me, and that they were strong.

I deployed, and, with the Ree scouts on my left, charged down the valley, driving the Indians with great ease for about 2½ miles. I, however, soon saw that I was being drawn into some trap, as they certainly would fight harder, and especially as we were nearing their village, which was still standing; besides, I could not see Custer or any other support; and at the same time the very earth seemed to grow Indians, and they were running toward me in swarms, and from all directions. I saw I must defend myself, and give up the attack mounted. This I did, taking possession of a point of woods, which furnished near its edge a shelter for the horses; dismounted, and fought them on foot, making headway through the woods. I soon found myself in the near vicinity of the village, saw that I was fighting odds of at least five to one, and that my only hope was to get out of the woods, where I would soon have been surrounded, and gain some high ground. I accomplished this by mounting and charging the Indians between me and the bluffs on the opposite side of the river. In this charge First Lieut. Donald McIntosh, Second Lieut. Benjamin H. Hodgson, and Acting Assistant Surgeon J. M. De Wolf were killed.

I succeeded in reaching the top of the bluff, with a loss of the three officers and 29 enlisted men killed, and seven men wounded. Almost at the same time I reached the top, mounted men were seen to be coming toward us, and it proved to be Capt. Benteen's battalion, Companies H, D, and K; we joined forces, and in a short time the pack train came up. As senior my command was then Companies A, B, D, G, H, K, and

M, about 380 men; and the following officers: Captains Benteen, Weir, French, and McDougall, First Lieutenants Godfrey, Mathey, and Gibson, Second Lieutenants Edgerly, Wallace, Varnum, and Hare, and A. A. Surgeon Porter. First Lieut. De Rudio was in the dismounted fight in the woods, but having some trouble with his horse did not join the command in the charge out, and hiding himself in the woods, joined the command after nightfall of the 26th.

Still hearing nothing of Custer, and with this reinforcement, I moved down the river in the direction of the village, keeping on the bluffs. We had heard firing in that direction, and knew it could only be Custer. I moved to the summit of the highest bluff, but seeing and hearing nothing, sent Capt. Weir, with his company, to open communication with the other command. He soon sent back word by Lieut. Hare that he could go no further, and that the Indians were getting around him. At this time he was keeping up a heavy fire from his skirmish line. I at once turned everything back to the first position I had taken on the bluff, and which seemed to me the best. I dismounted the men, had the horses and mules of the pack train driven together in a depression, put the men on the crests of the hills making the depression, and had hardly done so when I was furiously attacked. This was about 6 P.M. We held our ground, with the loss of 18 enlisted men killed and 46 wounded, until the attack ceased, about 9 P.M.

As I knew by this time their overwhelming numbers, and had given up any support from the portion of the regiment with Custer, I had the men dig rifle-pits; barricaded with dead horses, mules, and boxes of hard bread, the opening of the depression toward the Indians in which the animals were herded; and made every exertion to be ready for what I saw would be a terrific assault the next day. All this night the men were busy, and the Indians holding a scalp dance underneath us in the bottom and in our hearing.

On the morning of the 26th I felt confident that I could hold my own, and was ready as far as I could be, when at daylight, about 2:30 A.M., I heard the crack of two rifles. This was the signal for the beginning of a fire that I have never seen equaled. Every rifle was handled by an expert and skilled marksman, and with a range that exceeded our carbine; and it was simply impossible to show any part of the body, before it was struck. We could see, as the day brightened, countless hordes of them pouring up the valley from out the village, and scampering over the high points toward the places designated for them by their chiefs, and which entirely surrounded our position. They had sufficient numbers to completely encircle us, and men were struck on the opposite sides of the lines from which the shots were fired. I think we were fighting all the Sioux nation, and also all the desperados, renegades, half-breeds and squaw men, between the Missouri and the Arkansas and east of the Rocky Mountains. They must have numbered at least 2,500 warriors.

The fire did not slacken until about 9:30 A.M., and then we discovered that they were making a last desperate attempt, which was directed against the lines held by Companies H and M. In this attack they charged close enough to use their bows and arrows, and one man lying dead within our lines was touched by the "coup stick" of one of the foremost Indians. When I say the stick was only about 10 or 12 feet long, some idea of the desperate and reckless fighting of these people may be understood. This charge of theirs was gallantly repulsed by the men on that line led by Capt. Benteen. They also came close enough to send their arrows into the line held by Companies D and K, but were driven away by a like charge of the line, which I accompanied. We now had many wounded, and the question of water was vital, as from 6 P.M. of the previous evening until now, 10 A.M. (about 16 hours) we had been without it. A skirmish line was formed under Capt. Benteen, to protect the descent of volunteers down the hill in front of his position to reach the water.

We succeeded in getting some canteens, although many of the men were hit in doing so.

The fury of the attack was now over, and to my astonishment the Indians were seen going in parties toward the village. But two solutions occurred to us for this movement—that they were going for something to eat, more ammunition (as they had been throwing arrows), or that Custer was coming. We took advantage of this lull to fill all vessels with water, and soon had it by the camp kettle full; but they continued to withdraw, and all firing ceased, save occasional shots from sharpshooters, sent to annoy us about the water. About 2 P.M. the grass in the bottom was set on fire, and followed up by Indians who encouraged its burning, and it was evident it was done for a purpose, which purpose I discovered, later on, to be the creation of a dense cloud of smoke, behind which they were packing and preparing to move their tepees.

It was between 6 and 7 P.M. that the village came out from behind the clouds of smoke and dust. We had a close and good view of them, as they filed away in the direction of the Big Horn Mountains, moving in almost perfect military order. The length of the column was fully equal to that of a large division of the cavalry corps of the Army of the Potomac, as I have seen it on its march.

We now thought of Custer, of whom nothing had been seen and nothing heard since the firing in his direction about 6 P.M. on the eve of the 25th, and we concluded that the Indians had gotten between him and us, and driven him toward the boat, at the mouth of Little Big Horn River; the awful fate that did befall him never occurring to any of us as within the limits of possibilities. During the night I changed my position, in order to secure an unlimited supply of water, and was prepared for their return, feeling sure they would do so, as they were in such numbers. But early in the morning of the 27th, and while we were on the *qui vive* for Indians, I saw with my glass a dust some distance down the valley.

There was no certainty for some time what they were, but finally I satisfied myself they were cavalry, and if so could only be Custer, as it was ahead of the time that I understood that General Terry could be expected. Before this time, however, I had written a communication to Gen. Terry, and three volunteers were to try and reach him (I had no confidence in the Indians with me, and could not get them to do anything). If this dust were Indians, it was possible they would not expect any one to leave. The men started, and were told to go as near as was safe to determine if the approaching column was white men, and to return at once in case they found it so; but if they were Indians to push on to General Terry. In a short time we saw them returning over the high bluff already alluded to; they were accompanied by a scout who had a note from Terry to Custer, saying, "Crow scouts had come to camp saying he had been whipped, but it was not believed." I think it was about 10:30 A.M. that General Terry rode into my lines, and the fate of Custer and his brave men was soon determined by Capt. Benteen proceeding with his company to the battle ground.

The wounded in my lines were, during the afternoon and eve of the 27th, moved to the camp of General Terry; and at 5 A.M. of the 28th, I proceeded with the regiment to the battle ground of Custer, and buried 204 bodies, including the following named citizens: Mr. Boston Custer, Mr. Reed, and Mr. Kellogg. The following named citizens and Indians, who were with my command, were also killed: Charles Reynolds (guide and hunter) Isaiah; (colored) interpreter; Bloody Knife (who fell from immediately by my side); Bob-tailed Bull and Stab of the Indian scouts.

After following over his trail, it is evident to me that Custer intended to support me by moving further down the stream, and attacking the village in flank; that he found the distance to the ford greater than he anticipated; that he did charge, but his march had taken so long, although his trail shows he moved rapidly, that they were ready for him; that

Companies C and I, and perhaps part of Company E, crossed to the village or attempted it at the charge and were met by a staggering fire; and that they fell back to secure a position from which to defend themselves; but they were followed too closely by the Indians to permit him to form any kind of a line. I think had the regiment gone in as a body, and from the woods in which I fought advanced on the village, its destruction was certain; but he was fully confident they were running, or he would not have turned from me. I think (after the great number of Indians that were in the village) that the following reasons obtained for the misfortune: His rapid marching for two days and one night before the fight, attacking in the day time at 12 P.M. and when they were on the *qui vive*, instead of early in the morning; and lastly, his unfortunate division of the regiment into three commands.

During my fight with the Indians I had the heartiest support from officers and men, but the conspicuous services of Brevet Colonel F. W. Benteen, I desire to call attention to especially, for if ever a soldier deserved recognition by his government for distinguished services, he certainly does.

The harrowing sight of the dead bodies crowning the height on which Custer fell, and which will remain vividly in my memory until death, is too recent for me not to ask the good people of this country whether a policy that sets opposing parties in the field, armed, clothed, and equipped by one and the same government; should not be abolished. All of which is respectfully submitted.

The following is Capt. Benteen's account of his detour to the south and junction with Reno:

I was sent with my battalion to the left to a line of bluffs about five miles off, with instructions to look for Indians and see what was to be seen, and if I saw nothing there to go on, and when I had satisfied myself that it was useless to go further in that direction to rejoin the main trail. After proceeding through a rough and difficult country, very tiring on the horses, and seeing nothing, and wishing to save the horses unnecessary fatigue, I decided to return to the main trail. Before I had proceeded a mile in the direction of the bluffs I was overtaken by the chief trumpeter and the sergeant major, with instructions from Gen. Custer to use my own discretion, and in case I should find any trace of Indians, at once to notify Gen. Custer.

Having marched rapidly and passed the line of bluffs on the left bank of a branch of the Little Big Horn which made into the main stream about two and a half miles above the ford crossed by Col. Reno's command, as ordered, I continued my march in the same direction. The whole time occupied in this march was about an hour and a half. As I was anxious to regain the main command, as there was no signs of Indians, I then decided to rejoin the main trail, as the country before me was mostly of the same character as that I had already passed over, without valley and without water, and offering no inducement for the Indians. No valleys were visible, not even the valley where the fight took place, until my command struck the river.

About three miles from the point where Reno crossed the ford, I met a sergeant bringing orders to the commanding officer of the rear guard, Capt. McDougall, to hurry up the pack trains. A mile further I was met by my trumpeter, bringing a written order from Lieut. Cooke, the adjutant of the regiment, to this effect: "Benteen, come on; big village; be quick; bring packs:" and a postscript saying, "Bring packs." A mile or a mile and a half further on I first came in sight of the valley and Little Big Horn. About twelve or fifteen dismounted men were fighting on the plains with Indians, charging and recharging them. This body numbered about 900 at this time. Col. Reno's mounted party were retiring across the river to the bluffs. I did not recognize till later what part of the command this was, but was clear they had been beaten. I then marched my command in line to their succor.

On reaching the bluff I reported to Col. Reno, and first learned that the command had been separated and that Custer was not in that part of the field, and no one of Reno's command was able to inform me of the whereabouts of Gen. Custer. While the command was awaiting the arrival of the pack mules, a company was sent forward in the direction supposed to have been taken by Custer. After proceeding about a mile they were attacked and driven back. During this time I heard no heavy firing, and there was nothing to indicate that a heavy fight was going on, and I believe that at this time Custer's immediate command had been annihilated.

In a letter addressed to the *Army and Navy Journal*, Lieut. E. L. Godfrey, of Benteen's battalion, gives the following information:

Captain Benteen was some six miles from the scene of action when he received Lieut. Cooke's note; he had no intimation that the battle had begun, of the force of the Indians, or plan of attack. Benteen pushed ahead; the packs followed, and not until he reached the high bluffs overlooking the river valley and near to where the troops afterwards were beseiged, did he know of the battle or immediate presence of the troops to the enemy; he could only hear occasional shots, not enough to intimate that a battle was going on. Soon after reaching this point two volleys were heard down the river where Gen. Custer was, but his force was not in sight. Soon after this Reno and Benteen joined. By accident Benteen's column constituted a reserve. It was well it was so. As soon as dispositions were made on the bluff, Weir's company was sent to look for Gen.

Custer. He went to a high point about three-quarters of a mile down the river, from which he had a good view of the country. From it could be seen Custer's battle field, but there was nothing to indicate the result. The field was covered with Indians. He was recalled from the place; the packs closed up; ammunition was issued and the command moved down the river to, if possible, join Custer. Upon reaching this high point we could see nothing, hear nothing, to indicate Custer's vicinage. But immediately the Indians started for us.

The following is the narrative of George Herndon, a scout, published in the *New York Herald*:

At 11 P.M., June 24th, Custer followed the scouts up the right-hand fork of the Rosebud. About daylight we went into camp, made coffee, and soon after it was light the scouts brought Custer word that they had seen the village from the top of a divide that separates the Rosebud from Little Big Horn River. We moved up the creek until near its head, and concealed ourselves in a ravine. It was about three miles from the head of the creek where we then were to the top of the divide where the Indian scouts said the village could be seen, and after hiding his command, General Custer with a few orderlies galloped forward to look at the Indian camp. In about an hour he returned, and said he could not see the Indian village, but the scouts and a half-breed guide said they could distinctly see it some 15 miles off. Custer had "officers' call" blown, gave his orders, and the command was put in fighting order. The scouts were ordered forward, and the regiment moved at a walk. After going about three miles the scouts reported Indians ahead, and the command then took the trail.

Our way lay down a little creek, a branch of the Little Big Horn, and after going some six miles we discovered an Indian lodge ahead and Custer bore down on it at a stiff trot. In coming to it we found ourselves in a freshly-abandoned Indian camp, all the lodges of which were gone except the one we saw, and on entering it we found it contained a dead Indian. From this point we could see into the Little Big Horn valley, and observed heavy clouds of dust rising about five miles distant. Many thought the Indians were moving away, and I think Custer believed so, for he sent word to Reno, who was ahead, to push on the scouts rapidly and head for the dust. Reno took a steady gallop down the creek bottom three miles to where it emptied into the Little Big Horn, and found a natural ford across Little Big Horn River. He started to cross, when the scouts came back and called out to him to hold on, that the Sioux were coming in large numbers to meet him. He crossed over, however, formed his companies on the prairie in line of battle, and moved forward at a trot, but soon took a gallop.

The valley was about three-fourths of a mile wide. On the left a line of low, round hills, and on the right the river bottom, covered with a growth of cottonwood trees and bushes. After scattering shots were fired from the hills and a few from the river bottom, and Reno's skirmishers had returned the shots, he advanced about a mile from the ford, to a line of timber on the right, and dismounted his men to fight on foot. The horses were sent into the timber, and the men formed on the prairies and advanced toward the Indians. The Indians, mounted on ponies, came across the prairies and opened a heavy fire on the soldiers. After skirmishing for a few minutes Reno fell back to his horses in the timber. The Indians moved to his left and rear, evidently with the intention of cutting him off from the ford. Reno ordered his men to mount and move through the timber. Just as the men got into the saddle the Sioux, who had advanced in the timber, fired at close range and killed one soldier. Reno then commanded the men to dismount, and they did so; but he soon ordered them to mount again and moved out on the open prairie. The command headed for the ford, pressed closely by Indians in large numbers, and at every moment the rate of speed was increased, until it became a dead run for the ford. The Sioux, mounted on their swift ponies, dashed up by the side of the soldiers and fired at them, killing both men and horses. Little resistance was offered, and it was a complete route to the ford.

I did not see the men at the ford, and do not know what took place further than a good many were killed when the command left the timber. Just as I got out my horse stumbled and fell, and I was dismounted—the horse running away after Reno's command. I saw several soldiers who were dismounted, their horses having been killed or having run away. There were also some soldiers mounted who had remained behind. In all there was as many as 13 men, three of whom were wounded. Seeing no chance to get away, I called on them to come into the timber and we would stand off the Indians. They wanted to go out, but I said "No, we can't get to the ford, and, besides, we have wounded men and must stand by them." They still wanted to go, but I told them I was an old frontiersman, understood Indians, and, if they would do as I said, I would get them out of the scrape, which was no worse than scrapes I had been in before. About half of the men were mounted, and they wanted to keep their horses with them; but I told them to let them go, and fight on foot. We stayed in the bush about three hours, and I could hear heavy firing below in the river, apparently about two miles distant. I did not know who it was, but knew the Indians were fighting some of our men, and learned afterward it was Custer's command. Nearly all the Indians in the upper end of the valley drew off down the river, and the fight with Custer lasted about one hour, when the heavy firing ceased.

When the shooting below began to die away I said to the boys, "Come, now is the time to get out; the Indians will come back, and we had better be off at once." Eleven of the 13 said they would go, but two staid behind. I deployed the men as skirmishers, and we moved forward on foot toward the river. When we had got nearly to the river we met five Indians on ponies, and they fired on us. I returned the fire and the Indians broke, and we forded the river, the water being breast-deep. We finally got over, wounded men and all, and headed for Reno's command, which I could see drawn up on the bluffs along the river about a mile off. We reached Reno in safety. We had not been with Reno more than 15 minutes when I saw the Indians coming up the valley from Custer's fight. Reno was then moving his whole command down the ridge toward Custer. The Indians crossed the river below Reno and swarmed up the bluff on all sides. After skirmishing with them Reno went back to his old position which was on one of the highest points along the bluffs. It was now about 5 P.M., and the fight lasted until it was too dark to see to shoot. As soon as it was dark, Reno took the packs and saddles off the mules and horses and made breastworks of them. He also dragged the dead horses and mules on the line and sheltered the men behind them. Some of the men dug rifle pits with their butcher knives and all slept on their arms.

At the peep of day the Indians opened a heavy fire and a desperate fight ensued, lasting until 10 A.M. The Indians charged our position three or four times, coming up close enough to hit our men with stones, which they threw by hand. Captain Benteen saw a large mass of Indians gathering on his front to charge, and ordered his men to charge on foot and scatter them. Benteen led the charge, and was upon the Indians before they knew what they were about and killed a great many. They were evidently surprised at this offensive movement. I think in desperate fighting Benteen is one of the bravest men I ever saw. All the time he was going about through the bullets, encouraging the soldiers to stand up to their work and not let the Indians whip them. He never sheltered his own person once during the battle, and I do not see how he escaped being killed. The desperate charging and fighting was at about 1 P.M., but firing was kept up on both sides until late in the afternoon.

I think the Indian village must have contained about 6,000 people, fully 3,000 of whom were warriors. The Indians fought Reno first and then went to fight Custer, after which they came back to finish Reno. Hordes of squaws and old, gray-haired Indians were roaming over the battlefield howling like mad. The squaws had stone mallets, and mashed in the skulls of the dead and wounded. Our men did not kill any squaws, but the Ree Indian scouts did. The bodies of six squaws were found in the little ravine. The Indians must have lost as many men in killed and wounded as the whites did.

CHAPTER VII

KILL EAGLE'S NARRATIVE

A VIVID account of Custer's last battle has been given by an Indian named Kill Eagle, who was in Sitting Bull's village on the day of the fight as, he claims, a non-combatant. Kill Eagle was head chief of the Cheyenne River Agency Indians who had become much dissatisfied. Capt. Poland, formerly commander of the troops at Standing Rock, says that the Indians there were "abominably starved during the winter and spring of 1875—the authorities having failed to deliver the rations due them; and in May and June 1876, the Indians received practically nothing except two issues of beef and ground corn, called meal, but so coarse that one peck yielded but a quart of meal."

Early in May, Kill Eagle entered the military post with a party of warriors, gave a dance, demanded rations, and proclaimed "that he owned the land the post was built on, the timber and stone which had been used in its construction, and that he would have the Great Father pay for all these things; that his people were starving and they could get no food from the agent." The post commander told them he could do nothing for them. Kill Eagle's party manifested sulliness [*sic*], and demonstrated their defiance by firing off pistols in the air as they marched outside of the garrison. A few days later the post commander was informed that Kill Eagle had started for the hostile camp with about thirty lodges.

In September, Kill Eagle came near the post and sent word that he intended to kill all the soldiers unless they crossed the river. The troops were under arms all night anticipating an attack, but none was made. Subsequently Kill Eagle surrendered to the authorities, and gave them an account of his wanderings during the summer. A letter written at Standing Rock described his story as follows:

> He commences with the date at which he left this agency, last spring, with 26 lodges, for the purpose of hunting buffalo and trading with the hostile Indians. He speaks of having heard reports that troops were going out to punish the hostiles, but thought he would have time to do his hunting and trading and get out of the way before a battle occurred. They were obliged to hunt, as they were starving at the agency, and were very successful.
>
> On the seventh day they arrived at Sitting Bull's village, where a feast and numerous presents of ponies and robes were given them. Efforts were made to induce Kill Eagle and his band to join in the contemplated movements and hostilities, but evidently without much success. They were desirous of getting back again to the protecting arms of their agency, but were unable to escape from the meshes of the wily Sitting Bull. They found, too late, that for them there was no escape; their

horses were either shot or stolen, and wounds and insults were showered upon them from every side. In the meantime the forces of Crook were approaching, and with his people Kill Eagle succeeded in escaping temporarily from the hostiles. He claims to have been distant some forty or fifty miles from the scene of the Rosebud fight, and relates many of the incidents which he was able subsequently to gather from the participants. He places the loss of the Indians in the Rosebud fight at four dead, left on the field, and twelve that were brought to camp. He places the wounded at as high as 400, and says they had 180 horses killed, besides those that were captured.

He next comes to the fight on the Little Big Horn, and describes the Indian village, which was six miles long and one wide. He then speaks of Custer's approach and fight with its tragic details as an unwilling spectator, rather than a participant, who, during its progress, remained quietly in his lodge in the centre of the Indian village. The fight with Reno commenced about noon, the Indians all rushing to oppose his advance, until the approach of Custer toward the lower end of the village was announced, when the wildest confusion prevailed throughout the camp. Lodges were struck and preparations made for instant flight. Vast numbers of Indians left Reno's front and hastened to the assistance of their red brethren engaged with Custer, who was steadily forced back and surrounded until all were swept from the field by the repeated charges of the Indians.

He described the firing at this point as simply terrific, and illustrated its force by clapping his hands together with great rapidity and regularity. Then came a lull in the fearful storm of iron hail and his hands were still again. The storm beat fast and furious as the thought of some loved one nerved the arm of each contending trooper. Then the movement of his hands slackened and gradually grew more feeble. A few scattering shakes, like the rain upon a window pane, and then the movement ceased as the last of Custer's band of heroes went down with the setting sun.

It was dusk as the successful combatants returned to camp littered with their dead and wounded. "We have killed them all," they said, "put up your lodges where they are." They had just began to fix their lodges that evening, when a report came that troops were coming from toward the mouth of the creek. When this report came, after dark, the lodges were all taken down and they started up the creek. "I told my men," says Kill Eagle, "to keep together, and we would try and get away. Some one told on me, and they said let us kill him and his band, we have lost many young men to-day, and our hearts are bad. We travelled all night and next day; after crossing the Greasy Grass we encamped near the foot of the White Mountains. That night, when I was asleep, I heard a man calling. I woke up my people and this man proved to be a Cheyenne Indian, belonging to a party that had been off on the war-path in the White Mountains."

It was not to the Indians a bloodless victory. Fourteen had fallen in front of Reno, thirty-nine went down with Custer, and fourteen were dead in camp. Horses and travoises were laden with their wounded on every hand and in countless numbers. One band alone of Ogallallas had twenty-seven wounded on travoises, and thirty-eight thrown across horses. There were no white men in the fight or on the field. The bugle calls were sounded by an Indian. No prisoners were taken. The troops were all killed on the east side; none crossed the river.

Little Buck-Elk, an Uncapapa chief who came into Fort Peck in September, said that he was present at the fight with Custer, and that eleven different tribes were engaged in it. "The Indians were as thick as bees at the fight, and there were so many of them that they could not all take part in it. The soldiers were all brave men and fought well; some of them, when they found themselves surrounded and overpowered, broke through the lines and tried to make their escape, but were pursued and killed miles from the battle ground. The Indians captured six battle flags. No soldiers were taken alive, but after the fight the women went among the dead bodies and robbed and mutilated them. There were plenty of watches and money taken, which the young warriors are wearing in their shirts and belts."

CHAPTER VIII

AN ATTACK IN THE REAR

Major Reno's conduct on the first day of the fighting on the Little Big Horn, has been severely criticized by several of Gen. Custer's personal friends; and one of them, Gen T. L. Rosser, in a letter addressed to Reno and published in the *Army and Navy Journal*, blames him for taking to the timber when his "loss was little or nothing." "You had," he says, "an open field for cavalry operations, and I believe that if you had remained in the saddle and charged boldly into the village, the shock upon the Indians would have been so great that they would have been compelled to withdraw their attacking force from Custer, who, when relieved, could have pushed his command through to open ground, where he could have maneuvered his command, and thus greatly have increased his chances of success." It would seem as if this and similar criticisms were sufficiently answered by Reno's report; and by his reply to Rosser, which is given in part below:

After reading all your letter I could no longer look upon it as a tribute of a generous enemy, since through me you had attacked as brave officers as ever served a government, and with the same recklessness and ignorance of circumstances as Custer is charged with in his attacks upon the hostile Indians. Both charges—the one made against him and the one made by you against us—are equally untrue, You say: "I feel Custer would have succeeded had Reno, with all the reserve of seven companies, passed through and joined Custer after the first repulse;" and after confessing that you are firing at long range say further: "I think it quite certain that Custer had agreed with Reno upon a place of junction in case of the repulse of either or both detachments; and, instead of an effort being made by Reno for such a junction, as soon as he encountered heavy resistance he took refuge in the hills and abandoned Custer and his gallant comrades to their fate."

As I shall show, both the premises are false, and consequently all the conclusions of your letter fall to the ground. * * The only official orders I had from Custer were about five miles from the village, when Cooke gave me his orders in these words: "Custer says to move at as rapid a gait as you think prudent, and to charge afterwards, and you will be supported by the whole outfit."

No mention of any plan, no thought of junction, only the usual orders to the advance guard to attack by the charge. When the enemy was reached I moved to the front at a fast trot, and at the river halted ten minutes or less to gather the battalion. I sent word to Custer that I had the enemy in my front very strong, and then charged, driving the reds before me about three miles or less, to within a short distance of their village, supposing my command, consisting of 120 officers and men and about 25 scouts and guards, followed by the columns under Custer. The stream was very crooked, like a letter S in its wanderings, and on the side on which the village was it opened out into a broad bottom, perhaps half or three-quarters of a mile wide. The stream was fringed, as usual, with the trees of the plains—a growth of large cottonwood, and on the opposite side was a range of high bluffs which had been cut into very deep ravines.

As I neared the village the Indians came out in great numbers, and I was soon convinced I had at least ten to one against me, and was forced on the defensive. This I accomplished by taking possession of a point of woods where I found shelter for my horses. I fought there dismounted, and made my way to within 200 yards of the village, and firmly believe that if, at that moment, the seven companies had been together the Indians could have been driven from their village. As we approached near their village they came out in overwhelming numbers, and soon the small command would have been surrounded on all sides, to prevent which I mounted and charged through them to a position I could hold with the few men I had.

You see by this I was the advance and the first to be engaged and draw fire, and was consequently the command to be supported, and not the one from which support could be expected. All I know of Custer from the time he ordered me to attack till I saw him buried, is that he did not follow my trail, but kept on his side of the river and along the crest of the bluffs on the opposite side from the village and from my command; that he heard and saw my action I believe, although I could not see him; and it is just here that the Indians deceived us. All this time I was driving them with ease, and his trail shows he moved rapidly down the river for three miles to the ford, at which he attempted to cross into their village, and with the conviction that he would strike a retreating enemy. Trumpeter Martin, of Co. H, who the last time of any living person heard and saw Gen. Custer, and who brought the last order his adjutant ever penciled, says he left the General at the summit of the highest bluff on that side, and which overlooked the village and my first battle-field, and as he turned, Gen. Custer raised his hat and gave a yell, saying they were asleep in their tepees and surprised, and to charge. * * *

The Indians made him over confident by appearing to be stampeded, and, undoubtedly, when he arrived at the ford, expecting to go with ease through their village, he rode into an ambuscade of at least 2,000 reds. My getting the command of the seven companies was not the result of any order or prearranged plan. Benteen and McDougal arrived separately, and saw the command on the bluffs and came to it. They did not go into the bottom at all after the junction. They attempted to go down the trail of Gen. Custer, but the advance company soon sent back word they were being surrounded. Crowds of reds were seen on all sides of us, and Custer's fate had evidently been determined. I knew the position I had first taken on the bluff was near and a strong one. I at once moved there, dismounted, and herded the pack train, and had but just time to do so when they came upon me by thousands. Had we been twenty minutes later effecting the junction not a man of that regiment would be living to-day to tell the tale.

Another writer attacks both Reno and Benteen, accusing one of incapacity and utter demoralization during the attack of the Indians, and the other of wilful disobedience. "That he (Benteen) should have, as his own testimony confesses, deliberately disobeyed the *peremptory order of Custer* to 'Come on,' argues either a desire to sacrifice Custer, or an ignorance of which his past career renders him incapable. Custer told him to 'Come on,' and he reported to Reno." In order, as he says, to "vindicate the reputation of a noble man from unjust aspersions," this writer further declares, that "had Reno fought as Custer fought, and had Benteen obeyed Custer's orders, the battle of the Little Big Horn might have proved Custer's last and greatest Indian victory."

Of the writer last quoted, the *Army and Navy Journal* says: "With reckless pen he thrusts right and left, careless of reputations, regardless of facts, darkening the lives of other men, in the vain hope that one name may shine more brightly on the page of history * * * Nothing but the most absolute demonstration, accompanied by the proof, would justify such statements as he has made, and this he has not given. The reports of anonymous newspaper correspondents, and an *ex parte* statement of the conclusions drawn from letters, of which we have not so much as the names of the writers, is not proof on which to base criticisms affecting character and reputation."

Capt. Benteen, Brevet Colonel U.S.A., who has been a captain in the 7th Cavalry since its organization in 1866, at which date Gen. Custer was appointed its Lieut. Colonel, in a letter to the *Army and Navy Journal* uses the following language:

> Col. Reno and I thought during the seige of June 25th and 26th, at the Little Big Horn, that he, Reno, was the abandoned party, and spoke of it as another "Major Elliot *affair"; thinking that General Custer had retreated to the mouth of the river, where the steamboat was supposed to be, and that Reno's command was left to *its* fate. I am accused of disobeying Custer's orders. Nothing is further from the truth in point of fact; and I do not think the matter of sufficient importance to attempt to vindicate myself, but can rest contentedly under the ban when I have the consoling belief that the contrary is so well known by all my military superiors and comrades.

* Major Joel H. Elliot of the 7th Cavalry, and 19 of his command, were missing after the Battle of the Washita in Nov., 1868. Their dead bodies were found some weeks later.

Lieut. Gen. Sheridan, in his report for 1876, expresses his views of the Custer disaster as follows:

As much has been said in regard to the misfortune that occurred to General Custer and the portion of his regiment under his immediate command in this action, I wish to express the conviction I have arrived at concerning it. From all the information that has reached me, I am led to believe that the Indians were not aware of the proximity of Custer until he had arrived within about eight or nine miles of their village, and that then their scouts who carried the intelligence back to the valley were so closely followed up by Custer, that he arrived on the summit of the divide overlooking the upper portion of the village, almost as soon as the scouts reached it. As soon as the news was given, the Indians began to strike their lodges and get their women and children out of the way—a movement they always make under such circumstances. Custer, seeing this, believed the village would escape him if he awaited the arrival of the four companies of his regiment—still some miles in his rear. Only about 75 or 100 lodges or tepees could be seen from the summit or divide, and this, probably, deceived him as to the extent of the village. He therefore directed Major Reno, with three companies, to cross the river and charge the village, while he, with the remaining five companies, would gallop down the east bank of the river behind the bluff and cut off the retreat of the Indians. Reno crossed and attacked gallantly with his three companies—about 110 men—but the warriors, leaving the women to strike the lodges, fell on Reno's handful of men and drove them back to and over the river with severe loss.

About this time Custer reached a point about three and a half or four miles down the river, but instead of finding a village of 75 or 100 lodges, he found one of perhaps from 1500 to 2000, and swarming with warriors, who brought him to a halt. This, I think, was the first intimation the Indians had of Custer's approach to cut them off, for they at once left Reno and concentrated to meet the new danger. The point where Custer reached the river, on the opposite side of which was the village, was broken into choppy ravines, and the Indians, crossing from Reno, got between the two commands, and as Custer could not return, he fell back over the broken ground with his tired men and tired horses (they had ridden about 70 miles with but few halts) and became, I am afraid, an easy prey to the enemy. Their wild, savage yells, overwhelming numbers, and frightening war paraphernalia, made it as much as each trooper could do to take care of his horse, thus endangering his own safety and efficiency. If Custer could have reached any position susceptible of defence, he could have defended himself; but none offered itself in the choppy and broken ravines over which he had to pass, and he and his command were lost without leaving any one to tell the tale.

As soon as Custer and his gallant officers and men were exterminated and the scenes of mutilation by the squaws commenced, the warriors returned to renew the attack upon Reno; but he had been joined by Captain Benteen and the four companies of the regiment that were behind when the original attack took place, and the best use had been made of the respite given by the attack on Custer, to entrench their position.

Had the 7th Cavalry been kept together, it is my belief it would have been able to handle the Indians on the Little Big Horn, and under any circumstances it could have at least defended itself; but separated as it was into three distinct detachments, the Indians had largely the advantage in addition to their overwhelming numbers. If Custer had not come upon the village so suddenly, the warriors would have gone to meet him, in order to give time to the women and children to get out of the way, as they did with Crook only a few days before, and there would have been, as with Crook, what might be designated a rearguard fight—a fight to get their valuables out of the way, or in other words, to cover the escape of their women, children and lodges.

CHAPTER IX

THE MIDSUMMER CAMPAIGN

After regaining his position at the mouth of the Big Horn River, Gen. Terry called for reinforcements and additional troops were at once put in motion for his camp; but as they had to be collected from all the various stations on the frontier—some of them very remote from railroads—considerable time elapsed before their arrival.

During this period, the bands which had broken off from the main body of hostiles, and the young men at the agencies, continued their old and well-known methods of warfare, stealing horses on the frontier and killing small parties of citizens; while the constant communication by the hostiles with the Indians at the agencies made it evident that supplies of food and ammunition were being received. To prevent this, Gen. Sheridan deemed it necessary that the military should control the agencies, and at his request, the Secretary of the Interior, July 22d, authorized the military to assume control of all the agencies in the Sioux country.

About the same date Medicine Cloud, a chief, who had been sent from Fort Peck, in May, with a message to Sitting

Bull inviting him to visit Fort Peck with a view to reconciliation, returned to the agency. To the invitation, Sitting Bull had replied:

> Tell him I am coming before long to his post to trade. Tell him I did not commence. I am getting old, and I did not want to fight, but the whites rush on me, and I am compelled to defend myself. But for the soldiers stationed on the Rosebud, I with my people would have been there before that. If I was assured of the protection of the Great Father, I would go to Fort Peck for the purpose of making peace. I and others want the Black Hills abandoned, and we will make peace.

While awaiting reinforcements, Generals Terry and Crook were separated by about 100 miles of rough territory, the hostile Indians were between them, and for reliable communication with each other it was necessary to send around by the rear nearly 2000 miles. The carrying of dispatches direct was a work of the most arduous and perilous nature, and in doing it, and in reconnoitering, brave and gallant deeds were performed.

On the 6th of July, Gen. Crook sent out Lieut. Sibley of the 2nd Cavalry with 25 mounted troops and two guides, Gerard and Babtiste, to reconnoiter the country to the front, and learn if possible the movements of the enemy and the whereabouts of Terry's division. The party marched all night, and in the morning were near where the Little Big Horn debouches from the mountains. Here, from an eminence, they espied a large body of Indians marching eastward as though meditating an attack on the camp at Goose Creek. Concealing themselves as well as they could, they watched the movements of the enemy; but a great shout soon warned them that their trail had been discovered, and hundreds of savages immediately set out to follow it, uttering terrific cries.

The fugitives galloped toward the mountains, and seemed to outrun their pursuers; but about noon, while going through a ravine, a sudden volley was fired upon them from the surrounding slopes, and many Indians charged down upon them. They wheeled, and took refuge in the woods, but three horses were already wounded. Taking the ammunition from the saddles, and leaving their horses tied to the trees to divert the enemy, they now moved stealthily and unseen from the ground, and escaped behind adjacent rocks; then they climbed over steep and slippery places till exhausted, and while halting for a rest knew by the repeated firing that their horses were undergoing an attack.

All that night they toiled among the mountains, and on the morning of the 9th reached Tongue River. As they had left their rations behind, they suffered much from hunger, and two of the men were so weak they could not ford the deep stream, and remained behind. When near the camp one of the guides went ahead for assistance, and a company of cavalry brought in the exhausted men.

Having urgent occasion to communicate with Gen. Crook, Gen. Terry, by the promise of a large reward, induced a professional scout to make an attempt to reach him, but he soon returned unsuccessful. No other scout would undertake the task, and as a last resort a call for volunteers was made, in response to which, 12 soldiers promptly offered their services for the hazardous duty without hope of pecuniary reward. Three of these, Privates Wm. Evans, Benjamin F. Stewart, and Joseph Bell, of the 17th Infantry, were selected. They set out on the 9th of July, reached Crook's camp on the 12th; and returned on the 25th accompanied by three Crow Indians who had arrived from Terry's camp on the 19th. The three soldiers were thanked by their commander, in a General Order, "for a deed reflecting so much credit on the Service."

Partial reinforcements having reached Gen. Crook, on the 16th of July he broke camp and moved gradually along the hills toward Tongue River. On the 3d of August, just before sunset, an additional regiment, the 5th Cavalry, ten companies, under Col. W. Merritt, "marched into camp with their supply wagons close on their heels, presenting a fine appearance, despite the fatigue and dust of the march."

Gen. Crook's fighting force now numbered about 2000 men. Among them were over 200 Shoshone and Ute Indians, sworn enemies to the Sioux, led by Washakie, a well known Shoshone chief. These Indians were thus spoken of by a correspondent who saw them at Fort Bridger, drawn up in line before starting to join Gen. Crook:

> In advance of the party was a swarthy temporary chief, his face covered with vertical white streaks. In his right hand, hanging to the

end of a window-blind rod, were the two fingers of a dead Sioux. Another rod had a white flag nailed to it—a precaution necessary to preserve them from being fired upon in proceeding to the seat of war. The faces of the rest had on a plentiful supply of war paint. Once in line, they struck up a peculiar grunting sound on a scale of about five notes. One of the braves, afflicted with a malady peculiar to the Caucasian race, began to brag what he'd do when he got to the seat of war, winding up in broken English, "Me little mad now; bime [*sic*] by me heap mad." Old Washakie, their chief, wants to die in battle, and not in bed.

On the 5th of Aug., Gen. Crook cut loose from his wagon trains and started in pursuit of the Indians who, it was ascertained, had left the foot of the Big Horn Mountains, July 25th, and moved eastward. His route was north-easterly, across the Panther Mountains to Rosebud River. On the 8th of Aug. the troops were ten miles north of the battle-ground of June 17th, and near the site of a deserted village. The country west of the Rosebud had been burned over, and a trail recently traveled by large numbers of Indians led down the valley. Upon this trail the march was continued.

Meantime, Gen. Terry had been reinforced by six companies of the 5th Infantry under Col. Nelson A. Miles, six companies of the 22d Infantry under Lt. Col. Otis, and other detachments, until his command numbered about the same as Gen. Crook's. On the 25th of July, he started for the mouth of the Rosebud and there established a base of operations. On the 8th of Aug., with his troops and a train of 225 wagons with supplies for 30 days, he moved down the west bank of the Rosebud;

and on the 10th, when 35 miles from its mouth, made a junction with Crook's command. Col. Miles with the 5th Infantry was sent back to the mouth of the Rosebud to patrol the Yellowstone, aided by steamboats, and intercept the Indians should they attempt to cross the river.

The trail which Gen. Crook had been following now turned from the Rosebud eastward, and its pursuit was promptly and steadily continued by the united forces. It led the troops across to Powder River and down its valley. On the 17th of August they were encamped near the mouth of Powder River, on both sides of the stream; and here the two commands separated on the 24th of August.

As the principal Indian trail had turned eastward toward the Little Missouri, Gen. Crook's column took up the pursuit in that direction. On the 5th of Sept, when on the headwaters of Heart River, a small party of Indians were discovered going eastward, the first hostile Indians seen since leaving Tongue River.

The trail had now scattered so that it could be followed no longer, and Crook decided to push for the Black Hills settlements. His troops were nearly out of food, and suffering from want of clothing, and bad weather. Cold rains prevailed, and camp life with no tents, few blankets, and half rations, bore hard on the soldiers. Meat was scarce and some of the horses were killed to supply food.

On the 7th of Sept., Capt. Anson Mills with 150 men and a pack-train, was sent ahead with directions to obtain food at the Black Hills settlements about 100 miles distant, and to return to the hungry column as soon as possible. Gerard, the scout, accompanied the detachment, and on the evening of the 8th, he discovered a hostile village of 40 lodges and several hundred ponies. Capt. Mills retreated a few miles, hid his men in a ravine, and at day-break next morning dashed into the village. The Indians were completely surprised and fled to the surrounding hills, from which they exchanged shots with their assailants. The lodges were secured, with their contents consisting of large quantities of dried meat and other food, robes, and flags and clothing taken from Custer and his men. 140 ponies were also among the spoils.

A small party of the Indians had taken possession of a narrow ravine or canyon near the village, and in trying to dislodge them several soldiers were wounded. By direction of Gen. Crook, who had reached the field with reinforcements, the Indians in the ravine were informed that if they would surrender they would not be harmed. An old squaw was the first to take advantage of the offer, and was followed by 15 women and children, and, lastly, by three warriors, one of whom, the chief American Horse, had been mortally wounded.

Later in the day, before the troops had left the village, the Indians appeared in force and began a vigorous attack. Infantry were at once thrown out along the slope of the bluffs and, "about sundown it was a very inspiring sight to see this branch of the command with their long Springfield breech-loaders drive the enemy for a mile and a half to the west, and behind the castellated rocks." The captives in camp said the attacking Indians were reinforcements from the camp of Crazy Horse further west. This engagement is known as the battle of Slim Buttes. Our losses during the day were three killed, and 11 wounded including Lieut. Von Leuttroitz.

During the march of Sept. 10th a number of Indians came down on the rear, but were repulsed with a loss of several killed and wounded. Three soldiers were wounded in this skirmish.

The remainder of this long and difficult march was successfully accomplished. On the 16th, Gen. Crook reached Deadwood, a Black Hills settlement, and was cordially received by the inhabitants. In a speech made by the General on this occasion, he said:

> Citizens: while you welcome me and my personal staff as the representatives of the soldiers who are here encamped upon the Whitewood, let me ask you, when the rank and file pass through here, to show that you appreciate their admirable fortitude in bearing the sufferings of a terrible march almost without a murmur, and to show them that they are not fighting for $13 per month, but for the cause—the proper development of our gold and other mineral resources, and of humanity. This exhibition of your gratitude need not be expensive. Let the private soldier feel that he is remembered by our people as the real defender of his country.

After parting with Gen. Crook, Aug. 24th, Gen. Terry crossed the Yellowstone and marched down its left bank, his object being to intercept the Indians Crook was following if they attempted to cross the river. On the 27th he left the river, and moved northerly into the buffalo range where hunting parties were detailed who secured considerable game. The country was parched, the small streams dry, and water scarce. A scouting party made a detour to the north and west, but no Indians could be found. On the 5th of Sept. the whole command was at the mouth of Glendive Creek, where a military post had been established.

Gen. Terry now decided to close the campaign and distribute his troops to their winter quarters. The Montana column under Col. Gibbon started on the return march to Fort Ellis, 400 miles distant; Lieut. Col. Otis of the 22d Infantry, with his command, remained at Glendive Creek, to build a stockade and co-operate with Col. Miles, who was establishing a winter post at the mouth of Tongue River; and Gen. Terry with the balance of the troops started for Fort Buford at the mouth of the Yellowstone.

Hearing that Sitting Bull with a large band had recently crossed to the north side of the Missouri River near Fort Peck, Terry sent Reno with troops—then en route to Fort Buford—in pursuit. Reno marched to Fort Peck, and thence to Fort Buford, but encountered no Indians. A reconnoitering party under Long Dog had been near Fort Peck, and that chief passed one night at the agency. They did not want rations or annuities, but desired plenty of ammunition, for which they were ready to exchange 7th Cavalry horses, arms and equipments.

CHAPTER X

AUTUMN ON THE YELLOWSTONE

On the 10th of October, as a train escorted by two companies of the 6th Infantry was carrying supplies from Glendive Creek to the cantonment at the mouth of Tongue River, it was attacked by Indians, and was obliged to return to Glendive with a loss of sixty mules.

Lieut. Col. Otis was in command at Glendive, and on the 14th he again started out the train and personally accompanied it. The train consisted of 86 wagons, 41 of which were driven by soldiers, who had taken the places of as many citizen teamsters too demoralized by the recent attack to continue in the service. The military escort numbered with officers 196 men. The following interesting narrative of subsequent events is from the report of Col. Otis:

> We proceeded on the first day 12 miles, and encamped on the broad bottom of the Yellowstone River, without discovering a sign of the presence of Indians. During the night a small thieving party was fired upon by the pickets, but the party escaped, leaving behind a single pony, with its trappings, which was killed. At dawn of day, upon the 15th, the train

pulled out in two strings, and proceeded quietly to Spring Creek, distant from camp about three miles, when I directed two mounted men to station themselves upon a hill beyond the creek, and watch the surrounding country until the train should pass through the defile. The men advanced at swift pace in proper direction, and when within 50 yards of the designated spot, they received a volley from a number of concealed Indians, when suddenly men and Indians came leaping down the bluff. The men escaped without injury to person, although their clothing was riddled with bullets. I quickly advanced on the skirmish line, which drove out 40 or 50 Indians, and making a similar movement on the opposite flank, passed through the gorge and gained the high table land. Here, three or four scouts, sent out by Colonel Miles, from Tongue River, joined us. They had been driven into the Tongue upon the previous evening, there corraled, had lost their horses and one of their number, and escaped to the bluffs under cover of the darkness. The dead scout was found and buried.

The train proceeded along the level prairie, surrounded by the skirmish line, and the Indians were coming thick and fast from the direction of Cabin Creek. But few shots were exchanged, and both parties were preparing for the struggle which it was evident would take place at the deep and broken ravine at Clear Creek, through which the train must pass. We cautiously entered the ravine, and from 150 to 200 Indians had gained the surrounding bluffs to our left; signal fires were lighted for miles around, and extended far away on the opposite side of the Yellowstone. The prairies to our front were fired, and sent up vast clouds of smoke. We had no artillery, and nothing remained to us except to charge the bluffs. Company C, of the 17th Infantry, and Company H, of the 22d Infantry, were thrown forward upon the run, and gallantly scaled the bluffs, answering the Indian yell with one equally as barbarous, and driving back the enemy to another ridge of hills. We then watered all the stock at the creek, took on water for the men, and the train slowly ascended the bluffs.

The country now surrounding us was broken. The Indians continued to increase in numbers, surrounded the train, and the entire escort became engaged. The train was drawn up in four strings, and the entire escort enveloped it by a thin skirmish line. In that formation we advanced, the Indians pressing every point, especially the rear, Company C, 17th, which was only able to follow by charging the enemy, and then retreating rapidly toward the train, taking advantage of all the knolls and ridges in its course. The flanks, Companies G, 17th, and K and G, 22d, were advanced about 1000 yards, and the road was opened in the front, by Company H, 22d, by repeated charges.

In this manner we advanced several miles, and then halted for the night upon a depression of the high prairie, the escort holding the surrounding ridge. The Indians now had attempted every artifice. They had pressed every point of the line, had run their fires through the train, which we were compelled to cross with great rapidity, had endeavored to approach under cover of smoke, when they found themselves overmatched by the officers and men, who, taking advantage of the cover, moved forward and took them at close range. They had met with considerable loss, a good many of their saddles were emptied, and several ponies wounded. Their firing was wild in the extreme, and I should consider them the poorest of marksmen. For several hours they kept up a brisk fire and wounded but three of our men.

Upon the morning of the 16th, the train pulled out in four strings, and we took up the advance, formed as on the previous day. Many Indians occupied the surrounding hills, and soon a number approached, and left a communication upon a distant hill. It was brought in by Scout Jackson, and read as follows:

"Yellowstone."

"I want to know what you are doing traveling on this road? you scare all the buffalo away. I want to hunt on the place. I want you to turn back from here: if you don't I will fight you again. I want you to leave what you have got here, and turn back from here.

I am your friend, SITTING BULL.

I mean all the rations you have got and some powder; I wish you would write as soon as you can."

I directed the Scout Jackson to inform the Indians that I had nothing to say in reply, except that we intended to take the train through to Tongue River, and that we should be pleased to accommodate them at any time with a fight. The train continued to proceed, and about eight o'clock the Indians began to gather for battle.

We passed through the long, narrow gorge, near Bad Route Creek, when we again watered the stock, and took in wood and water, consuming in this labor about an hour's time. When we had pulled up the gentle ascent, the Indians had again surrounded us, but the lesson of the previous day taught them to keep at long range, and there was but little firing by either party. I counted 150 Indians in our rear, and from their movements and position I judged their numbers to be between 300 and 500. After proceeding a short distance, a flag of truce appeared on the left flank, borne by two Indians, whom I directed to be allowed to enter the lines. They proved to be Indian scouts from Standing Rock Agency, bearing dispatches from Lieut. Col. Carlin, of the 17th Infantry, stating that they had been sent out to find Sitting Bull, and to endeavor to influence him to proceed to some military post and treat for peace.

These scouts informed me that they had that morning reached the camp of Sitting Bull and Man-afraid-of-his-horse, near the mouth of Cabin Creek, and that they had talked with Sitting Bull, who wished to see me outside the lines. I declined the invitation, but professed a willingness to see Sitting Bull within my own lines. The scouts left me, and soon returned with three of the principal soldiers of Sitting Bull—the last named individual being unwilling to trust his person within our reach. The chiefs said that their people were angry because our train was driving away the buffalo from their hunting grounds, that they were hungry and without ammunition, and that they especially wished to obtain the latter; that they were tired of war, and desired to conclude a peace.

I informed them that I could not give them ammunition, that had they saved the amount already wasted upon the train it would have supplied them for hunting purposes for a long time, that I had no authority to treat with them upon any terms whatever, but they were at liberty to visit Tongue River, and there make known conditions. They wished to know what assurance I could give them of their safety should they visit that place, and I replied that I could give them nothing but the word of an officer. They then wished rations for their people, promising to proceed to Fort Rock [Peck] immediately, and from thence to Tongue River. I declined to give them rations, but finally offered them as a present 150 lb. of hard bread and two sides of bacon, which they gladly accepted. The train moved on, and the Indians fell to the rear. Upon the following day I saw a number of them from Cedar Creek, far away to the right, and after that time they disappeared entirely.

Upon the evening of the 18th I met Col. Miles encamped with his entire regiment on Custer Creek. Alarmed for the safety of the train, he had set out from Tongue River upon the previous day.

While Col. Otis was thus gallantly advancing with his train, Col. Miles, of the 5th Infantry, fearing for its safety, had crossed the Yellowstone before daybreak on the 17th and started toward Glendive. He met Col. Otis, as above stated, on the evening of the 18th; and on being informed of the attack on the train, started in pursuit of the enemy. On the 21st, when about eight miles beyond Cedar Creek, a large number of Indians appeared in front of the column, and two of them, bearing a white flag, rode up to the line. They proved to be the Standing Rock embassadors who had met Col. Otis; and brought word that Sitting Bull wished a conference with Col. Miles. Lieut. H. R. Bailey accompanied the two friendly Indians to the hostile camp, and there arranged with Sitting Bull's white interpreter for a meeting to take place between the lines.

The troops rested on their arms in line of battle while Col. Miles with a few officers rode forward and halted about half way between the two forces. Sitting Bull with a dozen unarmed warriors presently emerged from the hostile lines and walked slowly forward in single file. Col. Miles' party dismounted and advanced to meet them, and the council began. The scene was picturesque and exciting; and the occasion one of much anxiety to the troops who remembered the assassination of Gen. Canby—especially so when dozens of armed warriors rode forward and surrounded the little group.

The "talk" was long and earnest; the Indians wanted an "old-fashioned peace," with privileges of trade—especially in ammunition, and demanded the discontinuing of supply trains and the abandonment of Fort Buford. Col. Miles explained that he could only accept surrender on the terms of absolute submission to the U. S. Government. At evening the conference was adjourned to the next day, and the parties separated as quietly as they had assembled.

In the morning Col. Miles moved his command north, so as to intercept retreat in that direction. At about 11 A.M., Sitting Bull, Pretty Bear, Bull Eagle, John, Standing Bear, Gall, White Bull and others, came forward, marching abreast, and met Col. Miles and several officers on a knoll half way between the opposing lines. The Indians asked to be let alone, and professed a wish for peace, but such a peace as Col. Miles could not concede. "After much talk by the various chiefs, Sitting Bull was informed once and for all that he must accept the liberal conditions offered by the Government or prepare for immediate hostilities; and the council dispersed—Sitting Bull disappearing like a shadow in the crowd of warriors behind him."

The scene [wrote a correspondent of the *Army and Navy Journal*] was now most animated. Col. Miles sent for his company commanders, and they came charging over the field to receive his final instructions. On the other side, the Sioux leaders rode hither and thither at full speed in front of their line, marshaling their men and haranguing them, calling on them to be brave. Sitting Bull's interpreter, Bruey [Brughier], rode back to ask why the troops were following him? He was answered by Col. Miles, that the non-acceptance of the liberal terms offered was considered an act of hostility, and he would open fire at once. The whole line then advanced in skirmish order. One company occupied a knoll on the left with the 3-inch gun, the first shell from which was greeted with a hearty cheer from the advancing line. The Indians tried their old tactics and attempted rear and flank attacks from the ravines, but they found those vital points well protected by companies disposed *en potence*, which poured in a torrent of lead wherever an Indian showed himself. The firing then became general along the whole line. Some of the sharpest shooting was done by the Sioux, and many officers only escaped "close calls" by the ends of their hair. Two enlisted men were wounded. Finally, Sitting Bull, finding his old plan of battle frustrated by that solid infantry skirmish line advancing upon him with the relentless sternness of fate, began a general and precipitate retreat.

The pursuit was resolutely kept up. The Indians fled down Bad Route Creek and across the Yellowstone, a distance of 42 miles, abandoning tons of dried meat, lodge-poles, camp equipments, ponies, etc. The troops on foot followed rapidly, not stopping to count the dead or gather the plunder; and the result was, that on the 27th of October five principal chiefs surrendered themselves to Col. Miles, on the Yellowstone, opposite the mouth of Cabin Creek, as hostages for the surrender of their whole people, represented as between 400 and 500 lodges, equal to about 2,000 souls. The hostages were sent under escort to Gen. Terry, at St. Paul, and the Indians were allowed five days in their then camp to gather food, and thirty days to reach the Cheyenne Agency on the Missouri River, where they were to surrender their arms and ponies, and remain either as prisoners of war or subject to treatment such as is usually accorded to friendly Indians.

Sitting Bull was not among the chiefs who surrendered; during the retreat, they said, he had slipped out, with thirty lodges of his own special followers, and gone northerly.

CHAPTER XI

TERRY AND CROOK AT THE SIOUX AGENCIES

The disarming and dismounting of the Sioux Agency Indians being deemed necessary as a precautionary measure, to prevent the hostile Indians from receiving constant supplies of arms, ammunition, and ponies from their friends at the agencies, General Sheridan directed Generals Crook and Terry to act simultaneously in accomplishing that object. The friendly and unfriendly Indians at the agencies were so intermixed, that it seemed impossible to discriminate between them.

After refitting at the Black Hills, Gen. Crook proceeded to the Red Cloud Agency, and found the Indians there in a dissatisfied mood and probably about to start to join the hostile bands. They had moved out some 25 miles from the agency, and refused to return although informed that no more rations would be given them till they did so.

At daylight, Oct. 22d, Col. Mackenzie, the post commander, with eight companies of the 4th and 5th Cavalry, surrounded the Indian camp containing 300 lodges, and captured Red Cloud and his whole band, men, squaws and ponies without firing a shot, and marched them into the agency dismounted and disarmed. The Indians at Spotted Tail Agency were also disarmed and dismounted.

Gen. Crook had an interview with Spotted Tail, and being satisfied that he was the only important Sioux leader who had remained friendly, he deposed Red Cloud, and declared Spotted Tail, his rival, the "Sachem of the whole Sioux Nation, by the grace of the Great Father the President. As the representative of the latter, Gen. Crook invested him with the powers of a grand chief, and in token thereof presented him his commission as such, written upon a parchment scroll tied with richly colored ribbons. Spotted Tail's heart was very glad."

"The line of the hostile and the peacably disposed," wrote Gen. Crook at this time, "is now plainly drawn, and we shall have our enemies only in the front in the future. I feel that this is the first gleam of daylight we have had in this business."

Meantime Gen. Terry, with the 7th Cavalry and local garrisons, was disarming and dismounting the Indians at the Standing Rock and Cheyenne River Agencies. The following is a copy of his report to Gen. Sheridan, written at Standing Rock, Oct. 25th:

> Colonel Sturgis left Lincoln on the 20th, Major Reno on the 21st, and each arrived here on the afternoon of the 22d. Sturgis immediately commenced dismounting and disarming the Indians at Two Bears' camp, on the left bank of the river, and Lieut. Col. Carlin, with his own and Reno's forces, dismounted and disarmed them at both camps on this

side. Owing partially to the fact that before I arrived at Lincoln news was sent the Indians here, it is said, by Mrs. Galpin, that we were coming, and our purpose stated; but principally, I believe, that some time since, owing to the failure of the grass here, the animals were sent to distant grazing places many miles away, comparatively only a few horses were found. I, therefore, the next morning, called the chiefs together, and demanded the surrender of their horses and arms, telling them that unless they complied their rations would be stopped, and also telling them that whatever might be realized from the sale of the property taken would be invested in stock for them. They have quietly submitted, and have sent out to bring in their animals. Some have already arrived, and we have now in our possession 700. More are arriving rapidly, and I expect to double that number. I have kept the whole force here until now for the effect its presence produces.

I shall start Sturgis to-morrow morning for Cheyenne [River Agency], leaving Reno until Carlin completes the work here. Only a few arms have yet been found or surrendered, but I think our results are satisfactory. Not a shot was fired on either side of the river. Of course no surprise can now be expected at Cheyenne. The desired effect will be attained there by the same means as those employed here.

The late Sioux Commissioners, who made a treaty for the Black Hills in Sept. 1876, gave their pledge that all *friendly* Indians would be protected in their persons and property. Bishop Whipple comments on the dismounting of the Indians as follows:

In violation of these pledges 2,000 ponies were taken from Cheyenne and Standing Rock Agencies. No inventory was kept of individual property. Of 1,100 ponies taken at Standing Rock, only 874 left Bismarck for Saint Paul. No provision was made to feed them on the way. The grass had burned on the prairie and there was several inches of snow on the ground. The small streams, were frozen, and no water was to be had until they reached the James River. There was no grass, and no hay could be purchased until they reached the Cheyenne River, more than ten days travel, and then nothing until they reached Fort Abercrombie. No wonder that there were only 1,200 ponies out of 2,000 that left Abercrombie, and that of these only 500 reached St. Paul. The wretched, dying brutes were made the subject of jest as the war horses of the Dakota. Many died on the way, many were stolen, and the remnant were sold in St. Paul. It was worse than the ordinary seizure of property without color of law. It was not merely robbery of our friends. It was cruel. The Indians are compelled to camp from 10 to 40 miles away from the agency to find fuel. They have to cross this distance in the coldest weather to obtain their rations, and without ponies they must cross on foot, and some of them may perish.

Gen. Crook issued at Red Cloud Agency his General Orders, No. 8—in part as follows:

HEADQUARTERS DEPARTMENT OF THE PLATTE, IN THE FIELD
CAMP ROBINSON, NEB., Oct. 24th, 1876.

The time having arrived when the troops composing the Big Horn and Yellowstone Expedition are about to separate, the Brigadier-General commanding addresses himself to the officers and men of the command, to say:

In the campaign now closed he has been obliged to call upon you for much hard service and many sacrifices of personal comfort. At times you have been out of reach of your base of supplies; in most inclement weather you have marched without food and slept without shelter. In your engagements you have evinced a high order of discipline and courage, in your marches wonderful powers of endurance, and in your deprivations and hardships, patience and fortitude.

Indian warfare is, of all warfare, the most trying, the most dangerous, and the most thankless; not recognized by the high authority of the United States Congress as war, it still possesses for you the disadvantages of civilized warfare with all the horrible accompaniments that barbarians can invent and savages can execute. In it, you are required to serve without the incentive to promotion or recognition; in truth, without favor or hope of reward.

The people of our sparsely settled frontier, in whose defence this war is waged, have but little influence with the powerful communities in the East; their representatives have little voice in our national councils, while your savage foes are not only the wards of the nation, supported in idleness, but objects of sympathy with a large number of people otherwise well informed and discerning. You may, therefore, congratulate yourselves that in the performance of your military duty you have been on the side of the weak against the strong, and that the few people there are on the frontier will remember your efforts with gratitude.

Gen. Crook's losses during the campaign extending from May 27th to Oct. 24th, were 12 killed, 32 wounded (most of whom subsequently returned to duty), one death by accident and one by disease.

CHAPTER XII

THE WINTER OF 1876–77

AFTER leaving Red Cloud, Gen. Crook marched to Fort Fetterman and organized a new column for a winter expedition against the enemy. Subsequently, with a force of ten companies of cavalry under Col. Mackenzie, eleven companies of infantry and four of artillery under Lieut. Col. R. I. Dodge, and about 200 Indian allies, some of whom were friendly Sioux enlisted at Red Cloud Agency, Gen. Crook advanced to old Fort Reno, head of Powder River, where a cantonment had been built.

Hearing that a band of Cheyenne Indians were encamped among the Big Horn Mountains to the southwest, Gen. Crook, Nov. 23d, sent Col. Mackenzie with his cavalry and the Indian allies to hunt them up. At noon, Nov. 24th, after marching some 30 miles along the base of the mountains toward the Sioux Pass, Mackenzie met five of seven Indian scouts who had been sent ahead the evening previously. These scouts reported that they had discovered the camp of the Cheyennes at a point in the mountains about 20 miles distant, and that the other two scouts had remained to watch the camp.

A night's march was decided upon and, at sunset, after a halt of three hours, the command moved forward toward the village; but owing to the roughness of the country it was daylight when they reached the mouth of a canyon leading to and near the village. Through this canyon the column advanced, crossing several deep ravines, and when within a mile of the camp the order to charge was given. The Indian allies, who were in front, rushed forward howling and blowing on instruments, and some of them subsequently ascended the side of the canyon and occupied a high bluff opposite to and overlooking the village.

The surprise was nearly complete; but some of the Cheyennes, whom the scouts had reported as being engaged in a war dance, sounded the alarm on a drum, and began firing on the advancing column. The inhabitants immediately deserted their lodges, taking nothing but their weapons with them, and took refuge in a net-work of very difficult ravines beyond the upper end of the village. A brisk fight for about an hour ensued, after which skirmishing was kept up until night. The village of 173 lodges and their entire contents were destroyed, about 500, ponies were captured, and the bodies of 25 Indians killed in the engagement were found. Col. Mackenzie's loss was Lieut. J. A. McKinney and six men killed, and twenty-two men wounded.

On the 4th of Dec., Gen. Crook left Fort Reno with his whole force, and moved down Little Powder River, intending to form at its junction with Powder River a supply camp from which to operate against the Indians. Subsequently, however, he crossed over to the Belle Fourche River, and, Dec. 22d, started for Fort Fetterman where he arrived Dec. 29th. The weather during this homeward march was at times intensely cold, and the men and horses suffered considerably thereby.

While Gen. Crook was thus looking for and harassing the Indians in the Powder River country, the isolated garrison of the Tongue River cantonment, further north, were not idle. An excursion northward in search of Sitting Bull was led by Col. Miles, the post-commander, and as reports as to the location of the Indians were conflicting and their trails obscured by snow, he divided his force, and sent Lieut. Frank D. Baldwin with three companies of the 5th Infantry to the north of the Missouri, while he examined the Mussel Shell and Dry Forks country.

On the 7th of Dec., Lieut. Baldwin discovered Sitting Bull's band, and followed the Indians to the Missouri River, where they crossed and for a short time resisted the crossing of the troops. The Indians then retreated south, but were overtaken in the Redwood country and attacked, Dec. 18th. Their camp of 122 lodges was captured and burned with its contents, and 60 mules and horses were taken. The Indians escaped, but carried off little property except what they had on their backs.

Lieut. Baldwin's command marched on this expedition over 500 miles—walking on one occasion 73 miles in 48 hours—and endured the cold of a Montana winter with great fortitude.

A very unfortunate affair occurred at the Tongue River cantonment, within a few hundred yards of the parade-ground, Dec. 16th. The following is from Col. Miles' report thereof:

> As five Minneconjou chiefs were coming in, bearing two white flags, followed by twenty or thirty other Indians, and were passing by the Crow Indian camp, the five in advance were surrounded by twelve Crows and instantly killed. The act was an unprovoked, cowardly murder. The Crows approached them in a friendly manner, said "How," shook hands with them, and when they were within their power and partly behind a large wood pile, killed them in a most brutal manner. Upon hearing the first shot, both officers and men rushed out and tried to save the Minneconjous, but could not reach them in time. The Crows were aware of the enormity of their crime, as they saw that the Minneconjous had a flag of truce, and they were told to come back. They were warned the day before against committing any act of violence against messengers or other parties coming in for friendly purposes. They tried to hide the flag of truce and, taking advantage of the momentary excitement, while efforts were being made to open communication and bring back the others, who were following, and who became alarmed and fled to the bluffs, the guilty Crow Indians jumped upon their ponies and fled to their agency in Montana. The only thing that can be said in defence of the Crows is, that a false report was made by one of the Crow women that the Sioux had fired upon her, and that within the last few months some of their number had lost relatives killed by the Sioux in the vicinity of the Rosebud. These Indians have claimed

to be friends of the white man for years, have been frequently in the Government employ, and were brought down to fight such outlaws as Sitting Bull and Crazy Horse.

Those killed were believed to be Bull Eagle, Tall Bull, Red ——, Red Cloth, and one other prominent chief of the Sioux nation. I am unable to state the object of Bull Eagle's coming, but am satisfied he came with the best of motives. I can only judge from the following: When he surrendered on the Yellowstone, after the engagement on Cedar Creek, he was the first to respond to my demands, and, I believe, was largely instrumental in bringing his people to accept the terms of the Government. When I had received five of the principal chiefs as hostages, and was about parting with him, I told him, if he had any trouble in going in, or his people hesitated or doubted that the Government would deal fairly and justly with them, to come back to me, and I would tell him what to do; that if he would come back to my command, I would be glad to see him and, so long as he complied with the orders of the Government, he could be assured of the friendship of its officers. I could not but regard him with respect, as he appeared in every sense a chief, and seemed to be doing everything in his power for the good of his people, and endeavoring to bring them to a more peaceful condition. He appeared to have great confidence in what I told him; I gave him five days to obtain meat; during that time he lost three favorite ponies, which were brought to this place. During my absence he came in, bringing five horses that had strayed or been stolen from some citizens in the vicinity, and requested his own. He also inquired if he could send up to the Big Horn country for the remainder of his people, and take them in on the pass I had given him. He was informed by the commanding officer, Gen. Whistler (whom he had known for years before), that he could, and was told to send for them. Whether he had met with some trouble in taking his people in to their agency, and had returned, as I had told him, for directions, or had gathered up his people, and in passing had come in to apprise me of the fact, I know not; but there is every reason to believe that the above mentioned circumstances gave rise to his motives and prompted his actions.

The Crows were immediately disarmed, twelve of their ponies taken from them, and other considerations, together with a letter explaining the whole affair, were sent to the people and friends of those killed, as an assurance that no white man had any part in the affair, and that we had no heart for such brutal and cowardly acts.

It illustrates clearly the ferocious, savage instincts of even the best of these wild tribes, and the impossibility of their controlling their desire for revenge when it is aroused by the sight of their worst enemies, who have whipped them for years and driven them out of this country. Such acts are expected and considered justifiable among these two tribes of Indians, and it is to be hoped that the Sioux will understand that they fell into a camp of their ancient enemies, and did not reach the encampment of this command.

In January, 1877, Col. Miles with 350 of his troops marched southerly sixty miles up the Tongue River, and on the evening of the 7th discovered a large Indian village. Skirmishing ensued, and on the next day 1000 well-armed warriors appeared in front, and a battle was fought. The battle-ground was very rough and broken, and a heavy snow storm came on during the fight. The Indians fought with desperation; but our troops had been so admirably arranged that they succeeded in gaining a decisive victory. The following is Col. Miles' report of the affair:

I have the honor to report that this command fought the hostile tribes of Cheyenne and Ogallala Sioux, under Crazy Horse, in skirmishes on the 1st, 3d, and 7th of January, and in a five hours' engagement on the 8th inst. Their camp, consisting of some 500 lodges, extended three miles along the valley of Tongue River, below Hanging Woman's Creek. They were driven through the canyons of the Wolf or Panther Mountains, in the direction of Big Horn Mountains. Their fighting strength outnumbered mine by two or three to one, but by taking advantage of the ground we had them at a disadvantage, and their loss is known to be heavy. Our loss is three killed and eight wounded. They fought entirely dismounted, and charged on foot to within fifty yards of Captain Casey's line, but were taken in front and flank by Captain Butler's and Lieutenant McDonald's companies. They were whipped at every point and driven from the field, and pursued so far as my limited supplies and worn down animals would carry my command.

The following additional particulars are derived from a letter to the *Army and Navy Journal*:

On the 5th January, Indian signs grew thicker and thicker. Miles of hastily abandoned war lodges were passed. The country became very rough. The valley of the Tongue grew narrower, the stream more tortuous, and the hills on both sides loftier and more precipitous, until the valley shrank into a prolonged and winding canyon. At short distances, jutting bluffs made narrow passes which offered points of vantage to the savage enemy. The gorges of the Wolf Mountains had been reached.

On the 6th, the march was through a large war camp, recently and hurriedly abandoned. Unusual heat was followed by snow. In the evening there was snow and hail driven by a cruel wind, and by 5 P.M. it was pitch dark. On the evening of the 7th, the scouts captured four Cheyenne squaws, a youth, and three young children. Two hundred Indians made a dash at the scouts, shot two of their horses and made a desperate effort to take them. Casey opened a musketry fire on the Indians, and darkness supervening, they withdrew.

Next morning the fight was renewed shortly after daylight. The Indians charged down the valley in large force, close up to the skirmish line, but failed to make any impression. They then turned their attention to the flanks, and began to swarm on the bluffs to the right. The action then became general. The Indians were in strong force, and tried every point of the line. The hills and woods resounded with their cries and the high-pitched voices of the chiefs giving their orders.

It is the opinion of some who have had years of experience in Indian fighting, that there has rarely, if ever, been a fight before in which the Sioux and Cheyenne showed such determination and persistency, where they were finally defeated. They had chosen their ground; and it has since been learned that they expected to make another Custer slaughter. The Cheyenne captives, in the hands of the troops, sang songs of triumph during the entire fight, in anticipation of a speedy rescue and the savage orgies of a massacre.

In a complimentary order to his troops, dated Jan. 31st, Col. Miles says:

Here in the home of the hostile Sioux, this command, during the past three months, has marched 1200 miles and fought three engagements—besides affairs of less importance. * * * Fortunate indeed is the officer who commands men who will improvise boats of wagon beds, fearlessly dash out into the cold and turbid waters, and amid the treacherous current and floating ice, cross and recross the great Missouri; who will defy the elements on these bleak plains in a Montana winter; and who have in every field defeated superior numbers.

The dismounting and disarming policy was kept up at the Agencies through the winter. Several bands came in and surrendered—among them that of Red Horse, who had been actively hostile. This chief thus describes the engagement on the Little Big Horn. The "brave officer" referred to is said to be Capt. T. H. French, of Reno's battalion.

On the morning of the attack, myself and several women were out about a mile from camp gathering wild turnips. Suddenly one of the women called my attention to a cloud of dust rising in the neighborhood of the camp. I soon discovered that troops were making an attack. We ran for the camp, and when I got there I was sent for at once to come to the council-lodge. I found many of the council men already there when I arrived. We gave directions immediately for every Indian to get his horse and arms; for the women and children to mount the horses and get out of the way, and for the young men to go and meet the troops.

Among the troops was an officer who rode a horse with four white feet. The Indians have fought a great many tribes of people, and very brave ones, too, but they all say that this man was the bravest man they had ever met. I don't know whether this man was General Custer or not. This officer wore a large-brimmed hat and buckskin coat. He alone saved his command a number of times by turning on his horse in the retreat. In speaking of him, the Indians call him the "man who rode the horse with four white feet."

After driving this party back, the Indians corraled them on top of a high hill, and held them there until they saw that the women and children were in danger of being made prisoners by another party of troops which just then made its appearance below. The word passed among the Indians like a whirlwind, and they all started to attack the new party, leaving the troops on the hill. When we attacked the other party, we swarmed down on them and drove them in confusion. No prisoners were taken. All were killed. None were left alive even for a few minutes. These troopers used very few of their cartridges. I took a gun and a couple of belts off two dead men. Out of one belt two cartridges were gone; out of the other five.

It was with captured ammunition and arms that we fought the other body of troops. If they had all remained together they would have hurt us very badly. The party we killed made five different starts. Once we charged right in until we scattered the whole of them, fighting among them hand to hand. One band of soldiers was right in the rear of us when they charged. We fell back, and stood for one moment facing each other. Then the Indians got courage and started for them in a solid body. We went but a little distance when we spread out and encircled them. All the time I could see their officers riding in front, and hear them shouting to their men. We finished up the party right there in the ravine.

The troops up the river made their first attack, skirmishing a little while after the fight commenced with the other troops below the village. While the latter fight was going on we posted some Indians to prevent the other command from forming a junction. As soon as we had finished the fight we all went back to masacre the troops on the hill. After skirmishing around awhile we saw the walking soldiers coming. These new troops making their appearance was the saving of the others. An Indian started to go to Red Cloud Agency that day, and when a few miles from camp discovered dust rising. He turned back and reported that a large herd of buffalo was approaching the camp, and a short time after he reported this the camp was attacked by troops.

In February, Spotted Tail, with a body-guard of 200 warriors, started out to visit his roaming brethren as a peacemaker; and through his influence, or for other reasons, all the hostile bands, it is believed, except Sitting Bull's, have accepted the terms offered by the Government and surrendered their arms and ponies. One band of about 1000 encircled the Indian camp at Spotted Tail Agency, April 16th, and after discharging their guns in the air by way of salutation, surrendered to Gen. Crook. Roman Nose, whose village was destroyed at Slim Buttes, indicated his desire for peace in a short speech and by laying his rifle at the feet of the General. Five days later, 500 Cheyennes, with 600 ponies, came into Red Cloud Agency. Their village near Sioux Pass had been destroyed in November, and they were in a destitute and pitiable condition.

Crazy Horse and his band of 900 Indians surrendered at Red Cloud, May 5th. They appeared to be in a comfortable condition and had 2000 ponies.

At the latest date, Sitting Bull and his band were reported moving toward Canada. If they return south, Col. Miles will be prepared to give them a suitable reception.

CHAPTER XIII

A BIOGRAPHICAL SKETCH OF MAJOR-GENERAL CUSTER

George Armstrong Custer, son of Emmanuel H. Custer, a hard-working, enterprising farmer, was born at New Rumley, Harrison County, Ohio, December 5th, 1839. He grew up into an active, athletic, and amiable youth, acquired a fair English education, and at the age of sixteen years engaged in teaching school near his native town.

Having determined to go to West Point if possible, young Custer addressed a letter on the subject to Hon. John A. Bingham, Member of Congress from his district, to whom he was personally unknown, and subsequently called on him. The result was that he entered West Point Academy as a cadet in 1857. The official notification of his appointment was signed by Jefferson Davis, President Buchanan's secretary of war.

As a cadet, Custer did not achieve a brilliant record either for scholarship or good behavior. This was not owing to any want of intelligence or quickness of comprehension, but rather to a love of mischief and hatred of restraint. During the four years of his academic term he spent 66 Saturdays in doing extra guard duty as penance for various offences; and he graduated in 1861, at the foot of a class of 34.

His stay terminated with a characteristic incident. He chanced one day when officer of the guard to come upon two angry cadets, who from words had come to blows, and were just ready to settle their difficulty with their fists. Custer pushed through the crowd of spectators who surrounded the combatants, but instead of arresting them, as was his duty, he restrained those who were endeavoring to restrain them, and called out:

"Stand back, boys; let's have a fair fight."

His appeal was heard by Lieuts. Hazen and Merritt, and he was placed under arrest and kept back to be court-martialed, while the rest of his class, (excepting such as had already resigned to join the Southern army) departed for active service. The court-martial was however cut short, through the exertions of his fellow cadets at Washington, by a telegraphic order summoning him there.

Custer reported to the Adjutant-General of the Army at Washington, July 20th, and was by him introduced to Gen. Scott. The company (G, 2nd Cavalry) to which he had been assigned, with the rank of 2nd lieutenant, was at this time near Centerville, and as he was to join it, Gen. Scott entrusted to him some dispatches for Gen. McDowell who commanded the troops in the field. A night's ride on horseback took him to the army, the dispatches were delivered, and then he joined

General George A. Custer

his company before day-break just as they were preparing to participate in the battle of Bull Run. In this battle, however, the cavalry took but little part; in the frantic retreat that followed, Custer's company was among the last to retire, and did so in good order, taking with them Gen. Heintzelman who was wounded.

After Gen. McClellan took command of the army, Custer's company was attached to Gen. Phil Kearny's brigade, and that general detailed Custer as his aid-de-camp, and afterwards as assistant adjutant-general, which position he held till deprived of it by a general order prohibiting officers of the regular army from serving on the staffs of volunteer officers.

About this time he obtained leave of absence on account of ill health, and visited his sister, Mrs. Reed, at her home in Monroe, Michigan; and it is said that through her entreaties and influence he then gave up the habit of using strong drinks, which, in common with many of his fellow officers, he had acquired during his brief army life near Washington. Thenceforth, through the remainder of his life, he drank no intoxicating liquor.

Returning to the army in Feb. 1862, he was assigned to the 5th Cavalry, and when the enemy evacuated Manassas he participated in the advance on that place, and led the company which drove the hostile pickets across Cedar Run.

When the Army of the Potomac was transferred to the Peninsula, Custer's company was among the first to reach

Fortress Monroe, and it then marched to Warwick. Here he was detailed as assistant to the chief engineer, on Gen. W. F. Smith's staff; he served in that capacity during the siege of Yorktown, and planned the earthwork nearest the enemy's lines. At the battle of Williamsburg, where he acted as aid-de-camp to Gen. Hancock, he effected the capture of a battle-flag—the first taken by the Army of the Potomac.

When the army was encamped near the Chickahominy River, late in May, Custer accompanied Gen. Barnard, the chief engineer of the army, on a reconnoisance outside the picket line to the bank of the river; and at the request of his superior, he dismounted, jumped into the river, and waded across the stream—the object being to ascertain the depth of the water, which in some places came nearly up to his shoulders. On reaching the opposite bank he examined the ground for some distance, and discovered, unseen by them, the position of the enemy's pickets. Barnard reported to McClellan that the river was fordable, and how he had ascertained that it was so. McClellan sent for Custer, and was so pleased with his appearance and courageous act that he transferred him to his own staff; and in June, Custer received from the Secretary of War his appointment as additional aid-de-camp, with the rank of captain during the pleasure of the President. Previously to this he had crossed the Chickahominy at day-break with a company of infantry, attacked the enemy's picket post, and captured prisoners and arms.

Custer served on McClellan's staff through all of the Peninsular campaign; and after the battles of Gaines' Mills, Fair Oaks, Malvern Hill, etc., retreated with him to the protection of the gunboats at Harrison's Landing on the James River. Subsequently, after the withdrawal of the army from the Peninsula and the defeat of Banks and Pope in Virginia, he was McClellan's aid-de-camp in the Maryland campaign which closed with the battle of Antietam. When McClellan was superseded by Burnside, Nov. 10th, 1862, Custer accompanied his chief to Washington, and subsequently visited his friends in Ohio and Michigan. His staff position as captain ceased with the retirement of McClellan, and he was now a first lieutenant, commissioned July 17th, 1862.

In April, 1863, Custer rejoined his company which was with Gen. Hooker's army near Fredericksburg, and took part in the battle of Chancellorsville. In June he was on the staff of Gen. Pleasonton, then chief of the cavalry corps, and was conspicuous at Beverly Ford and other places across the Rappahannock where Stuart's cavalry were met and roughly handled.

At the battle of Aldie, Virginia, Custer distinguished himself in the charge made by Kilpatrick's cavalry. The onset was irresistible; the Confederate forces were driven back in confusion, and Custer's impetuosity carried him far within their lines, from which he was allowed to escape in consequence, he believed, of the similarity of his hat to those worn by the Confederates. For his gallantry in this action, Custer was promoted at one bound from a first lieutenant to a brigadier-general.

Gen. Custer was now assigned to the command of a Michigan brigade in Kilpatrick's division, the 1st, 5th, 6th and 7th Cavalry, and joined his command at Hanover, Md., June 29th. The next day he was engaged in a skirmish with Stuart's cavalry, and attracted the attention of all by the peculiarity of his dress. He wore a broad-brimmed, low-crowned felt hat; loose jacket and trowsers of velveteen, the former profusely trimmed with gold-braid and the latter tucked into high boots; a blue shirt, with turnover collar on either corner of which was an embroidered star; and a flaming neck-tie.

The battle of Gettysburg was now in progress, and on the 2nd of July Custer distinguished himself, and won the respect of his officers, by charging the enemy at the head of a company of his troops, having his horse shot under him. The next day his brigade was actively engaged, and the charge of the 1st Michigan Cavalry, supported by a battery, is designated by Custer as one of the most brilliant and successful recorded in the annals of warfare.

After the battle Gen. Lee retreated rapidly toward the Potomac, and the cavalry moving by different routes harassed him continually, capturing trains and prisoners. The following paragraph is copied from Headley's "History of the Civil War."

> Kilpatrick clung to the rebel army with a tenacity that did not allow it a moment's rest. At midnight, in a furious thunder storm, he charged down the mountain through the darkness with unparalleled boldness, and captured the entire train of Elwell's division, eight miles long. At

Emmettsburg, Hagerstown, and other places, he smote the enemy, with blow after blow. Buford, Gregg, Custer, and others, performed deeds which, but for the greater movements that occupied public attention, would have filled the land with shouts of admiration. In fact, the incessant protracted labors of the cavalry during this campaign, rendered it useless for some time.

Custer's brigade came upon the enemy's rear guard at Falling Waters, and the 6th Michigan made a gallant charge which was repulsed with considerable loss; but after a two hours' fight the enemy was driven to the river; Gen. Pettegrew and 125 of his men were killed, and 1500 were taken prisoners; cannon and battle-flags were also captured.

When the cavalry crossed the Rappahannock in September, pushing back Stuart's cavalry to Brandy Station, Culpepper C. H., and across the Rapidan, Custer, as usual, was with the advance, and in one engagement was slightly wounded by a piece of a shell—the first and only time he was wounded during the war. After a short vacation in consequence of his wound, he rejoined his command in season to accompany the advance of cavalry to and across the Rapidan in October; and when Meade's army was forced back across the Rappahannock, he assisted in covering the retreat. The following description of the engagement at Brandy Station is also copied from Headley:

Pleasonton, with the cavalry, remained behind to watch the enemy, and then slowly retired toward the retreating army. Buford had been forced back more rapidly than Kilpatrick, whose command—with Davis over the right brigade, and Custer over the left—fell back more slowly. When the latter reached Brandy Station, he found the former, ignorant of his movements, was far in advance, leaving his right entirely exposed. To make matters worse Stuart had passed around his left, so that Kilpatrick, with whom was Pleasonton himself, was suddenly cut off. The gallant leader saw at a glance the peril of his position, and, riding to a slight eminence took a hasty survey of the ground before him. He then gave his orders, and three thousand swords leaped from their scabbards, and a long, loud shout rolled over the field.

With a heavy line of skirmishers thrown out, to protect his flanks and rear, he moved in three columns straight on the rebel host that watched his coming. At first, the well-closed columns advanced on a walk, while the batteries of Pennington and Elder played with fearful precision upon the hostile ranks. He thus kept on, till within a few hundred yards of the rebel lines, when the band struck up "Yankee Doodle." The next instant, a hundred bugles pealed the charge, and away, with gleaming sabres and a wild hurrah, went the clattering squadrons. As they came thundering on, the hostile lines parted, and let them pass proudly through. Buford was soon overtaken, and a line of battle formed; for the rebels, outraged to think they had let Kilpatrick off so easy, reorganized, and now advanced to the attack.

A fierce cavalry battle followed, lasting till after dark. Pleasonton, Buford, Kilpatrick, Custer and Davis again and again led charges in person. It seemed as if the leaders on both sides were determined to test, on the plains of Brandy Station, the question of superiority between the cavalry; for the charges on both sides were of the most gallant and desperate character. The dark masses would drive on each other, through the deepening gloom, with defiant yells, while the flashing sabres struck fire as they clashed and rung in the fierce conflict. At length the rebels gave it up, and our cavalry, gathering up its dead and wounded, crossed the Rappahannock.

In the spirited encounter near Buckland's Mills, Oct. 19th, in which Stuart, aided by a flank attack from Fitz Hugh Lee, worsted Kilpatrick by force of numbers, Custer's brigade bore the brunt of the attack, and did most of the fighting on our side. This fight terminated the active campaign of 1863 for Custer's brigade, which subsequently guarded the upper fords of the Rapidan.

On the 9th of February, 1864, Gen. Custer was married at Monroe, Michigan, to Miss Elizabeth Bacon, only daughter of Judge Daniel S. Bacon of Monroe. When he rejoined his command at Stevensburg a few days later, his wife accompanied him, and she remained in camp till the opening of the spring campaign of 1864. The marriage was, as far as Custer was concerned, the consequence of love at first sight, and ever proved to be for both parties a happy one.

Late in February, 1864, Gen. Custer crossed the Rapidan with 1500 cavalry in light marching order, flanking Lee's army on the west, and pushed rapidly ahead to within four miles of Charlottesville, where he found his progress arrested by a far superior force. He then turned northward toward Stannardsville where he again encountered the enemy, and after skirmishing, returned to his camp followed by some hundreds of refugees from slavery. This raid was designed to draw attention from a more formidable one led by Kilpatrick at the same time.

CHAPTER XIV

A BIOGRAPHICAL SKETCH OF MAJOR-GENERAL CUSTER (*continued*)

In the spring of 1864, Gen. Grant was placed at the head of all the Union armies; Gen. Sheridan was called to command the cavalry corps in place of Gen. Pleasonton; and Custer with his brigade was transferred to the First division under Torbert.

In May, the Army of the Potomac once more advanced to the Rapidan and crossed it. In the battle of the Wilderness, owing to the character of the field, the cavalry were compelled to remain almost idle spectators, but subsequently, at Spottsylvania C. H., Torbert's division was seriously engaged.

On the 9th of May, Gen. Sheridan started out on his first great cavalry raid toward Richmond. At Beaverdam Station he inflicted great damage on the railroads, destroyed much property, and liberated 400 Union prisoners on their way to Richmond. Continuing his march, he found, at Yellow Tavern a few miles north of Richmond, Stuart's cavalry drawn up to oppose his passage. A spirited fight ensued, resulting in the death of Stuart and the dispersion of his troops. Our cavalry pressed on down the road to Richmond, and Custer's brigade attacked and carried the outer line of defenses, and took 100 prisoners. The second line of works was too strong to be taken by cavalry, and Sheridan was obliged to retreat. Beating off assailants both in front and rear he crossed the Chickahominy, pushed southward to Haxall's Landing on the James River, and then leisurely returned by way of White House and Hanover C. H. to Grant's army, arriving in time to be present at the sanguinary battle of Cool Arbor.

On the 9th of June, Custer accompanied Sheridan on a raid around Lee's army. They struck the railroad at Trevilian's, drove off a large force of the enemy and broke up a long section of the road. Retracing their steps to Trevilian's, they had there a spirited contest with Fitz Hugh Lee, and then drew off and rejoined Gen. Grant. During this raid Sheridan lost over 700 men, and captured 400 prisoners.

In the autumn of 1864, two divisions of cavalry under Torbert were with Sheridan's army operating in the Shenandoah Valley. Custer's brigade was in the First division, commanded by Merritt. Averill commanded the Second division.

Having received from Gen. Grant the order, "Go in"—the only instructions which Grant deemed it necessary to give—Sheridan, Sept. 19th, attacked the Confederate forces at Opequan Creek. The artillery opened along the whole line, the columns moved steadily forward, and Gen. Early soon discovered that Sheridan was in earnest. Early's position was a strong one, and he stubbornly held it until the cavalry bugles were heard on his right, as the firm-set squadrons bore fiercely down. Rolled up before the impetuous charge, the rebel line at length crumbled into fragments, and the whole army broke in utter confusion and was sent "whirling through Winchester," followed until dark by the pursuing cavalry. 3000 prisoners were taken.

Three days later Sheridan attacked Early at Fisher's Hill—a strong position to which he had retired—and again forced shim to retreat with a loss of 1100 men taken prisoners. The cavalry pursued so sharply and persistently, that Early left the valley and took refuge in the mountains where cavalry could not operate.

On the 26th of Sept., Custer was transferred from the command of the Michigan brigade in the First division to the head of the Second division; but before he was able to reach his new command, he was placed at the head of the Third division, with which he had formerly been connected under Kilpatrick.

When Sheridan moved back through the valley from Port Republic to Strasburg, sparing the houses, but burning all the barns, mills and hay-stacks, and driving off all the cattle, his rear was much harassed by the rebel cavalry under Gen. Rosser—a class-mate of Custer's at West Point; and on the night of Oct. 8th, Sheridan ordered Torbert to "start out at day-light, and whip the rebel cavalry or get whipped himself." Accordingly on the next morning the cavalry, led on by Merritt and Custer and supported by batteries, swept boldly out to attack a larger force drawn up in battle array. At the first charge upon them Rosser's men broke and fled, but subsequently rallied, and were again pushed back and utterly routed. Rosser lost all his artillery but one piece, and everything else which was carried on wheels, and was pursued to Mt. Jackson, 26 miles distant. Of this affair, Gen. Torbert reported:

> The First Division captured five pieces of artillery, their ordnance, ambulance, and wagon trains, and 60 prisoners. The Third Division captured six pieces of artillery, all of their headquarter wagons, ordnance, ambulance, and wagon trains. There could hardly have been a more complete victory and rout. The cavalry totally covered themselves with glory, and added to their long list of victories the most brilliant one of them all, and the most decisive the country has ever witnessed.

On the 15th of Oct., Sheridan started on a flying visit to Washington, leaving his army encamped on three ridges or hills. The crest nearest the enemy was held by the Army of West Virginia under Crook; half a mile to the rear of this was the second one, held by the 19th Corps under Emory; and still further to the rear, on the third crest, was the 6th Corps under Gen. Wright, who commanded the whole army during Sheridan's absence. The cavalry under Torbert lay to the right of the 6th Corps.

Gen. Early, having resolved to surprise and attack the Union army, started out his troops on a dark and foggy night, and advanced unperceived and unchallenged in two columns along either flank of the 6th Corps. The march was noiseless; and trusty guides led the steady columns through the gloom, now pushing through the dripping trees and now fording a stream, till at length, an hour before daybreak, Oct. 18th, Early's troops, shivering with cold, stood within 600 yards of Crook's camp. Two of Crook's pickets had come in at 2 A.M. and reported a heavy, muffled tramp heard at the front; but though some extra precautions were taken, no one dreamed that an attack would be made.

Crook's troops, slumbering on unconscious of danger, were awakened at day-break by a deafening yell and the crack of musketry on either flank; following which, charging lines regardless of the pickets came immediately on over the breast-works. The surprise was complete, and after a brief struggle the Army of West Virginia was flying in confusion toward the second hill occupied by the 19th Corps. Emory attempted to stop the progress of the enemy, but they got in his rear, and his command soon broke and fled with the rest toward the hill where the 6th Corps lay.

Gen. Wright formed a new line of battle, and repulsed a tremendous charge of the enemy, thus obtaining time to cover the immense crowd of fugitives that darkened the rear. A general retreat was then begun and continued in good order till 10 a.m. when, the enemy having ceased to advance, Wright halted and commenced reorganizing the scattered troops. The cavalry, being at the rear and extreme right, had not suffered in the first assault on the Union army, but they were subsequently transferred to the left flank, and did brave service in covering the retreat of the infantry.

Meanwhile Sheridan, returning from Washington, had slept at Winchester 20 miles distant, and in the morning rode leisurely toward his army. The vibrations of artillery at first surprised him, and he soon became aware that a heavy battle was raging and that his army was retreating. Dashing his spurs into his horse he pushed madly along the road, and soon left his escort far behind. Further on he met fugitives from the army, who declared that all was lost. As the cloud of fugitives thickened he shouted, as he drove on and swung his cap, "Face the other way, boys; we are going back to our camp; we are going to lick them out of their boots." The frightened stragglers paused, and then turned back.

On arriving at the front, where the work of reorganization was already well advanced, Sheridan inspired his men with new courage by his appearance and words. For two hours he rode back and forth in front of the line, encouraging the troops; and when the order was given, "The entire line will advance, etc.," the infantry went steadily forward upon the enemy. Early's front was soon carried, while his left was partly turned back; and after much desperate fighting, his astonished troops turned and fled in utter confusion over the field.

"As they streamed down into the Middletown meadow" [says Headley], "Sheridan saw that the time for the cavalry had come, and ordered a charge. The bugles pealed forth their stirring notes, and the dashing squadrons of Custer and Merritt came down like a clattering tempest on the right and left, doubling up the rebel flanks, and cleaving a terrible path through the broken ranks. Back to, and through our camp, which they had swept like a whirlwind in the morning, the panic-stricken rebels went, pellmell, leaving all the artillery they had captured, and much of their own, and strewing the way with muskets, clothing, knapsacks, and everything that could impede their flight. The infantry were too tired to continue the pursuit, but the cavalry kept it up, driving them through Strasburg to Fisher's Hill, and beyond, to Woodstock, sixteen miles distant."

After the battle of Cedar Creek and during the winter of 1864–5, Sheridan's army, including Custer's division, remained inactive, occupying cantonments around Winchester.

On the 27th of Feb., Sheridan started out on his last great raid, taking with him Gen. Merritt as chief of cavalry, the First and Third divisions of cavalry under Generals Devin and Custer, artillery, wagons, and pack-mules. The raiding column, including artillerymen and teamsters, numbered 10,000 men.

Moving rapidly up the Shenandoah Valley over the turnpike road, they passed many villages without halting or opposition, and on the 29th, approached Mount Crawford, where Rosser with 400 men disputed the passage over a stream and attempted to burn the bridge; but Col. Capehart of Custer's command, which was in advance, by a bold dash drove Rosser away and saved the bridge.

Custer now pushed on to Waynesboro' and finding Early intrenched there, immediately attacked him. The result, as told by Sheridan, was as follows:

> Gen. Custer found Gen. Early in a well chosen position, with two brigades of infantry, and some cavalry under Rosser, the infantry occupying breastworks. Custer, without waiting for the enemy to get up courage over the delay of a careful reconnoisance, made his dispositions for attack at once. Sending three regiments around the left flank of the enemy, Custer with the other two brigades, partly mounted and partly dismounted, at a given signal attacked and impetuously carried the enemy's works; while the Eighth New York and the First Connecticut cavalry, who were formed in columns of fours, charged over the breastworks, and continued the charge through the streets of Waynesboro', sabring a few men as they went along, and did not stop until they had crossed the South Fork of the Shenandoah, (which was immediately in Early's rear) where they formed as foragers, and with drawn sabres held the east bank of the stream. The enemy threw down their arms and surrendered, with cheers at the suddenness with which they had been captured.

Sixteen hundred prisoners, 11 pieces of artillery, 200 loaded wagons, and 17 battle-flags were captured single-handed by Custer at Waynesboro', while his own loss was less than a dozen men. Vast amounts of public property were subsequently destroyed. The prisoners were sent to Winchester under guard.

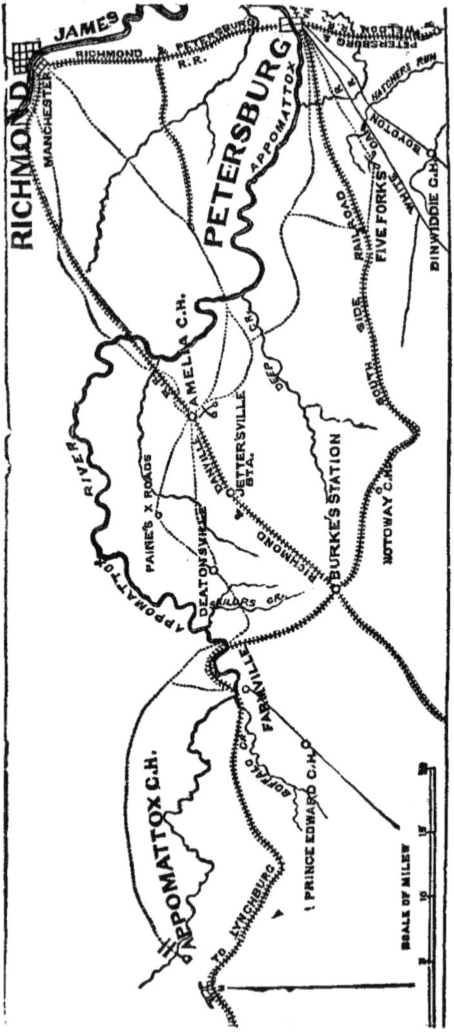
RICHMOND
JAMES
RICHMOND & PETERSBURG R.R.
MANCHESTER
PETERSBURG
APPOMATTOX
PETERSBURG & WELDON R.R.
HATCHERS RUN
BOYDTON
FIVE FORKS
DINWIDDIE C.H.
SOUTH SIDE RAIL ROAD
AMELIA C.H.
DEEP CR.
JETTER'SVILLE STA.
DANVILLE
RIVER
PAINE'S X ROADS
DEATONSVILLE
SAILORS CR.
BURKE'S STATION
RICHMOND
APPOMATTOX
FARMVILLE
BUFFALO CR.
PRINCE EDWARD C.H.
APPOMATTOX C.H.
TO LYNCHBURG
SCALE OF MILES

Pushing on across the Blue Ridge in a heavy rain during the night after Early's defeat, Custer, still in the van, approached Charlottesville the next afternoon, and was met by the authorities, who surrendered to him the keys of the public buildings as a token of submission. The balance of the column soon came up, and two days were spent in destroying bridges, mills, and the railroad leading to Lynchburg.

Sheridan now divided his command, and sent Merritt and Devin to destroy the canal from Scottsville to New Market, while he and Custer tore up the railroads as far west as Amherst C. H. The columns united again at New Market on the James River; and as the enemy had burned the bridges so they could not cross to the south side, they moved eastward behind Lee's army, destroying bridges, canals railroads and supplies, thus inflicting a more serious blow to the Confederate cause than any victories by land or sea gained during the last campaign. Then they swept around by the Pamunkey River and White House, and joined Grant's besieging army in front of Petersburg, March 27th. They encamped on the extreme left of the lines, close to their old comrades of the Second Division of cavalry, (now under Gen. Crook) who here again came under Sheridan's command.

CHAPTER XV

A BIOGRAPHICAL SKETCH OF MAJOR-GENERAL CUSTER (*continued*)

THE final struggle for the possession of Richmond and Petersburg was now commenced by an extension of the Union lines westward, Grant's object being to attack the right flank of the Confederates.

On the 29th of March, Sheridan, with his cavalry, moved southwest to Dinwiddie C. H., where Devin's and Crook's divisions halted for the night. Custer was some distance in the rear protecting the train. In the morning, Devin pushed the enemy back northerly to their intrenchments at Five Forks; but being unable to advance further, he returned to Dinwiddie C. H. Gen. Warren, with the 5th Infantry Corps, had meantime been put under Sheridan's command as a support to the cavalry, but had not yet come up.

The next day, 31st, Lee's troops attacked Warren unexpectedly, and drove two of his divisions back upon a third, where their advance was stopped; and with the assistance of Humphrey's 2nd Corps, the enemy were driven back into their entrenched position along the White Oak road. Then the rebel infantry moved westward along the road to Five Forks, and attacked Devin, who, earlier in the day, had advanced to Five Forks and carried that position. Devin was driven out in disorder and forced back, and after some difficulty rejoined Crook's division at Dinwiddie C. H. The confederates now assailed Sheridan with a superior force, but could make no headway, and during the night they withdrew.

Meantime Custer, and Gen. Mackenzie with 1,000 additional cavalry, had joined Sheridan, and Warren was within supporting distance. At day-break the cavalry advanced steadily on the enemy, and by noon had driven them behind their works at Five Forks, and were menacing their front. Warren was now ordered forward, and after more delay than Sheridan deemed necessary, he reached his assigned position and charged furiously westward on the enemy's left flank. Custer and Devin at the same time charged their right flank and front. Thus assailed by double their numbers the rebel infantry fought on with great gallantry and fortitude; but at length their flank defenses were carried by Warren's troops, and simultaneously the cavalry swept over their works. A large portion of the enemy surrendered, and the balance fled westward, pursued by Custer and Mackenzie; 5,000 prisoners were taken.

The next morning, Sunday, April 2nd, at day-break, a general assault was made by Grant's army upon the defences of Petersburg, and some of them were carried. Lee telegraphed to Davis that Richmond must be evacuated; and by night the Confederate rule in that city was ended, and Davis and his Government on the way by railroad to Danville. Lee's troops withdrew from Richmond and Petersburg the same night, and marched rapidly westward to Amelia C. H. on the Danville railroad, where they halted, April 4th and 5th, to gather supplies of food from the country.

Meantime, the Union army was pursuing the retreating Confederates and making every effort to prevent their escape. Custer and Devin moved southwesterly toward Burkesville destroying the railroad, and then joined Crook, Mackenzie, and the 5th Corps at Jetersville five miles west of Amelia C. H. Sheridan intrenched his infantry across the railroad, supported them by his cavalry, and felt prepared to stop the passage of Lee's whole army. Lee, however, finding his way to Danville thus blocked, moved northerly around Sheridan's left, and thence westerly toward Farmville on the Appomattox River. Gen. Davies, of Crook's division, made a reconnoisance and struck Lee's train moving ahead of his troops, destroying wagons, and taking prisoners. A fight followed, and Davies fell back to Jetersville where nearly the whole army was then concentrated.

On the morning of the 6th, Crook, Custer, and Devin started out in pursuit. Crook, who was in advance, was ordered to attack the trains, and if the enemy was too strong, another division was to pass him, while he held fast and pressed the enemy, and attack at a point further on—thus alternating until some vulnerable point was found. Crook came upon Lee's columns near Deatonsville, and charged upon them, determined to detain them at any cost. Crook was finally repulsed, but his action gave Custer time to push ahead, and strike further on at Sailor's Creek. Crook and Devin came promptly to Custer's support, and he pierced the line of march, destroyed 400 wagons, and took many prisoners. Elwell's division was separated from Lee, who was further ahead, and being enclosed between the cavalry in front and the infantry on their rear, the troops threw down their arms and surrendered.

That evening Lee crossed the Appomattox at Farmville, and tried to burn the bridges behind him, but troops arrived in season to save one of them. Lee halted five miles beyond Farmville, intrenched himself, and repulsed an attack from the infantry. At night he silently resumed his retreat.

On the morning of the 7th, Custer and Devin, under Merritt, were sent on a detour to the left, to cut off retreat toward Danville should it be attempted; while Crook forded the Appomattox and attacked a train. On the 8th, Sheridan concentrated the cavalry at Prospect Station, and sent Merritt, Custer, and Devin swiftly ahead 28 miles to Appomattox Station, where, he had learned from scouts, were four trains loaded with supplies for Lee, just arrived from Lynchburg.

Gen. Custer took the lead, and on reaching the railroad station he skillfully surrounded and captured the trains. Then, followed by Devin, he hurried on five miles further to Appomattox C. H., where he confronted the van of Lee's army, immediately attacked it, and by night had turned it back on the main column, and captured prisoners, wagons, guns, and a hospital train. The balance of the cavalry hurried up, and a position was taken directly across the road, in front of Lee's army.

By a forced march the infantry under Griffin and Ord, supporting the cavalry, reached the rear of Sheridan's position by day-break the next morning. Grant and Mead were pressing closely on Lee's rear, and Lee saw there was no escape for him unless he could break through the cavalry force which he supposed alone disputed his passage. He therefore ordered his infantry to advance. The result of this charge, the last one made by the Army of Virginia, is thus described in Greeley's "*American Conflict*":

> By Sheridan's orders, his troopers, who were in line of battle dismounted, gave ground gradually, while showing a steady front, so as to allow our weary infantry time to form and take position. This effected, the horsemen moved swiftly to the right, and mounted, revealing lines of solid infantry in battle array, before whose wall of gleaming bayonets the astonished enemy recoiled in blank despair, as Sheridan and his troopers, passing briskly around the rebel left, prepared to charge the confused, reeling masses. A white flag was now waved by the enemy before Gen. Custer, who held our cavalry advance, with the information that they had concluded to surrender.

The next day, April 9th, Gen. Custer, who had been brevetted Major-General after the battle of Cedar Creek, issued the following complimentary order to his troops:

HEAD-QUARTERS THIRD CAVALRY DIVISION.
APPOMATTOX COURT HOUSE, VA., April 9, 1865.

SOLDIERS OF THE THIRD CAVALRY DIVISION:

With profound gratitude toward the God of battles, by whose blessings our enemies have been humbled and our arms rendered triumphant, your Commanding General avails himself of this his first opportunity to express to you his admiration of the heroic manner in which you have passed through the series of battles which to-day resulted in the surrender of the enemy's entire army.

The record established by your indomitable courage is unparalleled in the annals of war. Your prowess has won for you even the respect and admiration of your enemies. During the past six months, although in most instances confronted by superior numbers, you have captured from the enemy, in open battle, 111 pieces of field artillery, 65 battle-flags, and upward of 10,000 prisoners of war including seven general officers. Within the last ten days, and included in the above, you have captured 46 field-pieces of artillery and 37 battle-flags. You have never lost a gun, never lost a color, and have never been defeated; and notwithstanding the numerous engagements in which you have borne a prominent part, including those memorable battles of the Shenandoah, you have captured every piece of artillery which the enemy has dared to open upon you. The near approach of peace renders it improbable that you will again be called upon to undergo the fatigues of the toilsome march, or the exposure of the battle-field; but should the assistance of keen blades wielded by your sturdy arms be required to hasten the coming of that glorious peace for which we have been so long contending, the General Commanding is firmly confident that, in the future as in the past, every demand will meet a hearty and willing response.

Let us hope that our work is done, and that blessed with the comforts of peace, we may be permitted to enjoy the pleasures of home and friends. For our comrades who have fallen, let us ever cherish a grateful remembrance. To the wounded and to those who languish in Southern prisons, let our heartfelt sympathy be tendered.

And now, speaking for myself alone, when the war is ended and the task of the historian begins; when those deeds of daring which have rendered the name and fame of the Third Cavalry Division imperishable are inscribed upon the bright pages of our country's history, I only ask that my name may be written as that of the Commander of the Third Cavalry Division.

Lee's flag of truce at Appomattox—a white towel—and also the table on which Grant and Lee signed the capitulation agreement, were presented to Mrs. Custer by Gen. Sheridan, and are now in her possession. In a letter accompanying them Sheridan wrote, that he "knew of no person more instrumental in bringing about this most desired event than her own most gallant husband."

In the great parade of the Army of the Potomac at Washington in May 1865, Sheridan's cavalry were at the head of the column; and the Third Division, first in peace as it had been first in war, led the advance. Custer, now a Major-General of volunteers, at the age of 26 years, rode proudly at the head of his troopers, a prominent figure in the stirring pageant, and the observed of all beholders. He had put off for the occasion his careless dashing style of dress, and wore, with becoming dignity, the full regulation uniform of a Major-General.

Shortly after the parade, Custer was sent to Texas, where he had command of a cavalry division at Austin, but no active

service became necessary. In March, 1866, he was mustered out of service as a Major-General, and took rank as a Captain, assigned to the 5th Cavalry, U.S.A. Soon afterward, he applied to Senor Romero, Minister from Mexico, for a position as chief of President Juarez's cavalry, in his struggle with Maximilian. He presented a letter of introduction from General Grant in which he was spoken of in the most complimentary terms. Romero was anxious to secure his services, and made him liberal offers; but as Custer could not obtain leave of absence from his Government, the contemplated arrangement was not completed.

CHAPTER XVI

A BIOGRAPHICAL SKETCH OF MAJOR-GENERAL CUSTER (*continued*)

IN July, 1866, Custer received from Andrew Johnson, a commission as Lieut. Col. of the 7th Cavalry—a new regiment; and after accompanying the President on his famous tour through the country, he proceeded to Fort Riley, Kansas.

In the spring of 1867, an expedition under Gen. Hancock marched from Fort Riley to Fort Larned near the Arkansas River, and the 7th Cavalry, under Lieut. Col. Custer, accompanied it. The dissatisfied Indians had been invited by the Indian agent to meet Hancock in council at Fort Larned, and had agreed to do so; but as they failed to appear at the appointed time, Hancock started for a village of Sioux and Cheyenne Indians, distant some 30 miles from the fort. On the way he met several of the chiefs, and they agreed to hold a council at Hancock's camp on the next day, April 14th. As none of the chiefs came, as promised, Hancock again started for their village, and soon came upon several hundred Indians drawn up in battle array directly across his path. The troops were immediately formed in line of battle, and then the General, with some of his officers and the interpreter, rode forward and invited the chiefs to a meeting between the lines, which were half a mile apart. The invitation was accepted; several chiefs advanced to the officers, and a friendly interview was holden—all seeming pleased at the peaceful turn things had taken. The result of the "talk" was an arrangement for a council to be held at Hancock's headquarters after he had camped near the Indian village, toward which both parties then proceeded. It was ascertained on reaching it that the women and children had been sent away; and during the night the warriors, unobserved by the white men, also fled, leaving their lodges and stores.

Mistrusting something of the kind, Custer, with the cavalry, had during the night stealthily surrounded the village, and on entering it later found it deserted. Pursuit of the Indians was commenced, but their trail soon scattered so it could not be followed. After burning the deserted village, the expedition returned to Fort Hayes, where the 7th Cavalry wintered.

The next summer, Custer with several companies of his regiment and 20 wagons, was sent on a long scouting expedition to the southward in search of Indians. Leaving Fort Hayes in June, he proceeded to Fort McPherson on the Platte River, and thence to the forks of the Republican River in the Indian country. From this place he sent Major J. H. Elliott, on the 23d of June, with ten men and one guide, to carry despatches to Gen. Sherman at Fort Sedgwick, 100 miles distant. The wagons, escorted by cavalry, were also started the same day to procure supplies from Fort Wallace, about the same distance away in an opposite direction.

Early the next morning, an attack was made on the camp, but the soldiers rallied so promptly and effectively that the Indians soon withdrew. Interpreters were then sent toward them, who arranged for a council which was held near by. After an unsatisfactory interview, Custer returned to his camp and started in pursuit of the Indians, but was unable to overtake them.

On the fifth day after his departure, Major Elliott returned in safety to the camp. He had traveled only by night, and had seen no Indians. The wagon train was not so fortunate. It reached Fort Wallace safely, and started to return escorted by 48 troopers. On the way it was attacked by a large number of Indians, who for three hours kept up a running fight around the circle. The wagons moved forward in two strings, with the cavalry horses between them for safety, and the dismounted soldiers defended them so successfully that their progress forward was uninterrupted. Meanwhile Custer, fearing for the safety of the train, had sent out cavalry to meet it; and their approach caused the Indians to cease from their attack and withdraw. The balance of the journey was safely accomplished.

Resuming his march, Custer again struck the Platte, some distance west of Fort Sedgwick. Here he learned by telegraph that Lieut. Kidder with ten men and an Indian scout had started from Fort Sedgwick, with despatches for Custer directing him to proceed to Fort Wallace, shortly after Major Elliott had left the fort. As Kidder had not returned and Custer had not seen him, fears for his safety were entertained, and Custer immediately started for his late camp at the forks of the Republican. On the way thither some of his men deserted, and being followed and refusing to surrender, were fired upon, and three were wounded.

On reaching the camp, an examination was made by the Indian guide, and it was ascertained that Kidder's party had arrived there in safety, and continued on towards Fort Wallace, over the trail made by the wagons. In the morning Custer started in pursuit, and by noon it became evident by the tracks of their horses, that Kidder's party had been hard chased for several miles. Further on one of their horses was found, shot dead; and at last the mutilated and arrow-pierced bodies of the 12 men were found lying near each other. They had been chased, overtaken, and killed by the savages. They were buried in one grave, and the troops proceeded to Fort Wallace.

Custer had been ordered to report to Gen. Hancock at Fort Wallace, and receive further orders from him; but on arriving there he found that the General had retired to Fort Leavenworth. The location of Fort Wallace was isolated and remote from railroads, and as the stock of provisions was low, Custer decided to go for supplies. He started on the evening of July 15th, with 100 men, and arrived at Fort Hayes on the morning of July 18th, having marched 150 miles, with a loss of two men who had been surprised by Indians. He then proceeded to

Fort Harker, 60 miles further on, and after making arrangements for the supplies, obtained from Gen. Smith permission to visit his wife, who was at Fort Riley, 90 miles distant by rail.

Soon after this Custer was arraigned before a court-martial, charged with leaving Fort Wallace without orders, and making a journey on private business, during which two soldiers were killed; also for over-tasking his men on the march, and for cruelty while quelling a mutiny. After trial, he was pronounced guilty of a breach of discipline in making a journey on private business (which he earnestly denied) and acquitted of the other charges. His sentence was a suspension of pay and rank for a year, during which period he remained in private life, while his regiment was engaged in an expedition under Gen. Sully.

In October, 1868, Custer was recalled into service, and joined his regiment at Fort Dodge on the Arkansas River. Early in Nov., a winter campaign against the Indians was commenced. Gen. Sully, with the 7th Cavalry, detachments of infantry, and a large supply train, marched to the borders of the Indian country and established a post called Camp Supply.

On the 23d of Nov., Custer with his regiment of about 800 men started out in a snow storm on a scout for the enemy. The next day a trail was discovered and pursued, and at night the troops were in the valley of the Washita River, and near an Indian village which had been seen from a distance. The village was stealthily surrounded, and at daybreak an attack was made simultaneously by several detachments.

The Indians were taken entirely by surprise. The warriors fled from the village, but took shelter behind trees, logs, and the bank of the stream, and fought with much desperation and courage, but were finally driven off. The village was captured with its contents, including 50 squaws and children who had remained safely in the lodges during the fight. Some 800 ponies were also captured. On questioning the squaws, one of them said that she was a sister of the Cheyenne chief Black Kettle, that it was his village that had been captured, and that several other Indian villages were located within ten miles—the nearest one being only two miles distant.

Before Custer had time to retreat, hostile Indians—reinforcements from the other villages—arrived in such numbers as to surround the captured village, which Custer and his men occupied; and an attack was begun which continued nearly all day. The Indians were finally driven away. The village and its contents were burned. The captives were allowed to select ponies to ride on, and the balance of the drove were shot. The retreat was begun by a march forward, as if to attack the next village. The Indians fled; and after dark Custer moved rapidly back toward Supply Camp, taking the captives along as prisoners of war.

In this engagement, known as the Battle of the Washita, Major Elliott, Capt. Hamilton, and 19 privates were killed, and three officers and 11 privates wounded. Captains Weir, Benteen, T. W. Custer, and Lieut. Cook, participated in this fight. It was estimated that at least 100 Indians were killed, among whom was the noted chief Black Kettle.

The death of Black Kettle was much regretted by many white people. Gen. Harney said respecting him: "I have worn the uniform of my country 55 years, and I know that Black Kettle was as good a friend of the United States as I am." Col. A. G. Boone, a member of the recent Indian Commission, who had known Black Kettle for years, said tearfully: "He was a good man; he was my friend; he was murdered."

Early in Dec., the 7th Cavalry and a Kansas cavalry regiment, accompanied by Gen. Sheridan and staff, again started out to look for Indians. The recent battle-ground was revisited, and then the force proceeded along the valley of the Washita, finding the sites of several villages which appeared to have been lately and hastily removed. Large numbers of lodge poles, and robes, utensils, and stores were left behind; and a broad trail, leading down the river toward Fort Cobb, 100 miles distant, showed the direction their owners had taken when frightened away from their winter retreat. A pursuit of the trail was commenced, but it soon branched. The troops continued on, and when within 20 miles of Fort Cobb, Indians appeared in front with a flag of truce. They proved to be Kiowas led by Lone Wolf, Satanta, and other chiefs.

A council was held, and both parties agreed to proceed together to Fort Cobb; and the Indians agreed that they would then remain on their reservation. On the way to the fort, many of the Indians slipped away, and as Custer then supposed (erroneously) that Lone Wolf and Satanta had been engaged in the recent battle and might also escape, he placed them under guard and took them to Fort Cobb, where they were held as hostages for the return of the roaming Kiowas, who finally came in on learning that Sheridan had determined to hang their chiefs if they failed to do so.

Soon after this, Little Robe—a Cheyenne chief, and Yellow Bear—a friendly Arapahoe, were visiting at Fort Cobb, and at Custer's suggestion Sheridan permitted him with a small party to go with these chiefs as a peace embassador. The mission was successful as far as the Arapahoes were concerned, and as its result the whole tribe returned to their reservation.

The effort to arrange with the Cheyennes proving unavailing, Custer with 800 men started, March, 1869, in pursuit of them. On the 13th of March he arrived in the vicinity of several Cheyenne villages, one of which belonged to Little Robe. Several councils were held with the chiefs; and it was ascertained that two white women who had been recently captured in Kansas were held as captives in one of the villages. For this reason Custer could not attack the Indians, who were still intractable, and had to continue negotiations with them. They refused to release the women unless a large ransom was paid.

Custer subsequently seized four of the chiefs, and threatened to hang them if the white women were not given up unconditionally. This threat produced the desired effect, and the

women were surrendered. Custer then marched to the supply camp, taking with him the captured chiefs, who begged for freedom as the white women had been given up. Their friends also entreated for their release; but Custer assured them that the Washita prisoners and the captive chiefs would not be liberated until the Cheyennes returned to their reservation. This they promised to do, and subsequently kept their word.

CHAPTER XVII

A BIOGRAPHICAL SKETCH OF MAJOR-GENERAL CUSTER (*continued*)

A TREATY having been made with the Indians and peace restored, the 7th Cavalry enjoyed a long season of rest. In the autumn of 1870, it was broken into detachments and distributed to different posts. Custer, with two companies, was assigned to a post at Elizabethtown, Ky., 40 miles from Louisville, and in this isolated place he remained two years. During this period of inaction he engaged in literary pursuits and wrote an account of his life on the Plains. He also joined in a buffalo-hunt given on the Plains in honor of the Russian Grand Duke Alexis, and after the hunt he and Mrs. Custer accompanied the Duke in his travels through the Southern States.

In March, 1873, the 7th Cavalry was ordered to Dakota, and in May was encamped at Fort Rice far up the Missouri. Here also were assembled other soldiers, and in July the so-called Yellowstone Expedition, commanded by Gen. D. S. Stanley, started out on its mission, which was to escort and protect the engineers and surveyors of the Northern Pacific Rail-road. The march was westward to the Yellowstone and up its valley, accompanied part of the way by steamboats. The country was rough and broken, and the wagon trains were got forward with much difficulty. It was Custer's custom to go ahead every day with a small party of road-hunters, to pick out and prepare the most suitable road for the train.

On the 4th of Aug., when opposite the mouth of Tongue River, as Custer and his advance party of about 100 men were enjoying a noon-day siesta in a grove on the bank of the river, they were aroused by the firing of the pickets. A few Indians had made a dash to stampede the horses which were grazing near by, and failing in this, were riding back and forth as if inviting pursuit. The soldiers speedily mounted, and Custer with 20 men followed the Indians, who retreated slowly, keeping out of the reach of shot.

After going nearly two miles the retreating Indians faced about as if to attack, and simultaneously, 300 mounted warriors emerged from a forest and dashed forward. Custer's men immediately dismounted, and while five of them held the horses, the remainder, with breech-loading carbines, awaited the enemy's charge. Several rapid volleys were sufficient to repulse the Indians, and cause them to take shelter in the woods from which they came.

Just then the remainder of Custer's men came up, and the whole force retreated to the resting place they had so lately vacated. The horses were sheltered in the timber, and the men took advantage of a natural terrace, using it as a breastwork.

The Indians had followed them closely, and now made persistent but unsuccessful attempts to drive them from their position. Being defeated in this, they next tried to burn them out by setting fire to the grass. After continuing their assault for several hours, the Indians withdrew at the approach of the main column, and Custer and the fresh troops chased them several miles.

The same day, two elderly civilians connected with the expedition were murdered while riding in advance of the main column. Nearly two years later, Charles Reynolds, a scout subsequently killed at the battle of the Little Big Horn, while at Standing Rock Agency, heard an Indian who was "counting his *coups*," or in other words rehearsing his great achievements, boast of killing two white men on the Yellowstone. From his description of the victims and the articles he exhibited, Reynolds knew that he was the murderer of the two men.

The name of this Indian was Rain in the Face. He was subsequently arrested by Captains Yates and Custer, and taken to Fort Lincoln where he was interviewed by Gen. Custer and finally confessed the deed. He was kept a close prisoner in the guard-house for several months, but managed to escape, and joined Sitting Bull's band. It is thought by some that he was the identical Indian who killed Gen. Custer, and that he did it by way of revenge for his long imprisonment. There seems to be no real foundation for this theory; but the "Revenge of Rain in the Face" will probably go down to posterity as an

historical truth, as it has already been immortalized in verse by one of our most gifted poets, who seems, however, to have overlooked the fact that Gen. Custer's body was not mutilated.

A week after the affair on the Yellowstone a large Indian trail was discovered leading up the river, and Custer was sent in pursuit. On arriving near the mouth of Big Horn River, it was discovered that the enemy had crossed the Yellowstone in "bull boats." As Custer had no means of getting across, he camped for the night. Early the next morning he was attacked by several hundred warriors, some of whom had doubtless recrossed the river for that purpose. Sitting Bull was commander of the Indians, and large numbers of old men, squaws, and children were assembled on the high bluffs and mounds along the river to witness the fight. After considerable skirmishing Custer ordered his troops to charge, and as they advanced the Indians fled, and were pursued some distance.

In these two engagements our loss was four men killed, and two were wounded. Custer's horse was shot under him. There was no further trouble with the Indians, and the expedition returned to Fort Rice about the 1st of October. Later in the autumn, Gen. Custer was assigned to the command of Fort Lincoln, on the Missouri River, opposite the town of Bismarck.

In the summer of 1874, a military expedition to explore the Black Hills was decided on, and Gen. Custer was selected to command it. The column of 1,200 troops, escorting a corps of scientists, etc., started from Fort Lincoln, July 1st, moved southwesterly about 250 miles to the Black Hills, and then explored the region. No trouble was experienced with Indians, and the expedition returned to Fort Lincoln in September.

Mrs. Custer had accompanied her husband to the Plains when he first went thither, and excepting when he was engaged in some active campaign or both were East, she shared with him the hardships, privations, and pleasures of frontier life. Mrs. Champney, speaking of her in the *Independent*, says: "She followed the general through all his campaigns, her constant aim being to make life pleasant for her husband and for his command. General Custer's officers were remarkably attached to him; to a man they revered and admired his wife. She was

with him not only in the idleness of summer camp-life, when the days passed in a *dolce far niente* resembling a holiday picnic; but in ruder and more dangerous enterprises she was, as far as he would permit, his constant companion."

When Gen. Custer was ordered to Fort Lincoln Mrs. Custer went there with him; that retired post was their home for the remainder of his life, and when he started out on his last campaign she parted with him there.

CHAPTER XVIII

A BIOGRAPHICAL SKETCH OF MAJOR-GENERAL CUSTER (*continued*)

When a campaign against the roaming hostile Indians was decided on in 1876, Lieut. Col. Custer was naturally selected as the leader of the Dakota column, which was organized at Fort Lincoln, and mainly composed of his regiment.

About this time a Congressional committee at Washington were investigating the charges against Gen. Belknap, who had recently resigned the office of Secretary of War. Many persons were called to testify; and while Custer was actively engaged in organizing the Sioux expedition, he received a telegraphic summons to appear before the committee.

On the receipt of the summons, Custer telegraphed to Gen. Terry, the Department Commander, informing him of the fact, stating that what he knew as to any charges against the War Department was only from hearsay evidence, and asking his advice as to what he had better do. Terry, who was a lawyer as well as a soldier, in reply informed Custer that his services were indispensable, and that he feared it would delay the expedition if he had to go to Washington. He suggested that if Custer knew nothing of the matter, he might perhaps get excused from going there.

After hearing from Terry, Custer telegraphed to the chairman of the committee as follows:

> While I hold myself in readiness to obey the summons of your committee, I telegraph to state that I am engaged upon an important expedition, intended to operate against the hostile Indians, and I expect to take the field early in April. My presence here is very necessary. In view of this, would it not be satisfactory for you to forward to me such questions as may be necessary, allowing me to return my replies by mail.

As the committee would not consent to the plan proposed, Custer went to Washington, and was detained there on this business about one month. He was severely cross-examined, but the result showed that he knew but little of the matter in controversy. All he could say of his own knowledge was, that a contractor had turned over to him at Fort Lincoln a quantity of grain, which he suspected had been stolen from the Indian Department, as the sacks bore the Indian brand. He had at first refused to receive the grain, and had informed the Department commander of his suspicions. He had received in reply an order to accept the grain; and he believed that the order emanated from the Secretary of War, and so testified before the committee. On returning west, he learned from Gen. Terry that he alone was responsible for the order to receive the grain; and thereupon, Custer telegraphed the fact to Mr. Clymer, and added: "As I would not knowingly do injustice to any individual, I ask that this telegram may be appended to and made part of my testimony before your committee."

On being discharged by the committee, Custer, for the third time it is said, called at the White House, hoping to remove the wrong impression and misunderstanding as to his action before the committee which, he had learned from private sources, the President had received and still entertained. He did not however succeed in getting an interview, and it is said that Gen. Grant even refused to see him.

Leaving the White House, Custer proceeded to the office of Gen. Sherman, and learned that the General had gone to New York, but was expected back that evening. Custer then took the train for Chicago, and on arriving there was halted by Gen. Sheridan who had received from Gen. Sherman a telegram dated May 2nd, as follows:

> I am this moment advised that General Custer started last night for Saint Paul and Fort Abraham Lincoln. He was not justified in leaving without seeing the President or myself. Please intercept him at Chicago or Saint Paul, and order him to halt and await further orders. Meanwhile let the expedition from Fort Lincoln proceed without him.

Gen. Custer was of course greatly surprised on learning that such a telegram had been received, and he immediately telegraphed to Gen. Sherman a statement of the circumstances under which he left Washington. He reminded the General that at their last interview he had stated that he would start west May 1st, and had been told in reply that it was the best thing he could do; he said further that he had every reason to believe, that in leaving Washington when he did he was acting in accordance with the General's advice and wishes; and in conclusion, he reminded the General of his promise that he should go in command of his regiment, and asked that justice might be done him. Receiving no answer to this message, he again telegraphed to Sherman asking as a favor that he might proceed to Fort Lincoln where his family was. In reply, Sherman telegraphed as follows:

> Before receipt of yours, I had sent orders to Gen. Sheridan, to permit you to go to Fort Lincoln on duty, but the President adheres to his conclusion that you are not to go on the expedition.

Sherman's orders to Sheridan were as follows:

> I have received your despatch of to-day, announcing Gen. Custer's arrival. Have just come from the President, who orders that Gen. Custer be allowed to rejoin his post, to remain there on duty, but not to accompany the expedition supposed to be on the point of starting against the hostile Indians, under Gen. Terry.

General Custer accordingly started for Fort Lincoln, and on arriving at Saint Paul, May 6th, he addressed the following letter to President Grant:

> To His Excellency the President, through Military Channels:
>
> I have seen your order transmitted through the General of the army, directing that I be not permitted to accompany the expedition about to move against hostile Indians. As my entire regiment forms a

part of the proposed expedition, and as I am the senior officer of the regiment on duty in this Department, I respectfully but most earnestly request that while not allowed to go in command of the expedition, I may be permitted to serve with my regiment in the field. I appeal to you as a soldier to spare me the humiliation of seeing my regiment march to meet the enemy and I not to share its dangers.

This appeal to the President was forwarded by Gen. Terry with the following communication:

> In forwarding the above, I wish to say expressly, that I have no desire to question the orders of the President, or of my military superiors. Whether Lieut. Col. Custer shall be permitted to accompany my column or not, I shall go in command of it. I do not know the reasons upon which the orders already given rest; but if those reasons do not forbid it, Lieut. Col. Custer's services would be very valuable with his command.

It may be well to state here the probable causes of the unfriendly feeling which Gen. Grant at this period manifested toward one whom he had "endorsed to a high degree" ten years previously. The Congressional committee hitherto mentioned, had been appointed by the Opposition members of the House, and some of its proceedings had, doubtless, annoyed and vexed the President. Gen. Babcock had been on his staff during the war, and enjoyed his friendship and support even after the damaging disclosures respecting the sale of the post-tradership at a western fort. Attempts had also been made about this time to injure Grant's administration, by seeking to identify it with the frauds which had been discovered, or which were suspected, and he naturally considered those who volunteered information to the committee as unfriendly to himself.

It was currently reported that Custer telegraphed to the committee's chairman, that an investigation into the post-traderships upon the Upper Missouri would reveal a state of things quite as bad as at Fort Sill; and that in consequence of this communication he was summoned before the committee.

But whatever the causes of Gen. Grant's unfriendliness, or the cruelty charged upon him for showing his displeasure as he did, the result of Gen. Custer's appeal was creditable to the President. Custer resumed his position as Terry's trusted coadjutor in fitting out the expedition, and finally marched from Fort Lincoln as commander of his regiment. It was no disgrace to him that Terry accompanied the column, and the best feeling always existed between the two officers. The junction with the Montana troops was contemplated at the time, and their commander, Col. Gibbon, would have ranked Lieut. Col. Custer when their forces united. Some commanding general had usually accompanied previous expeditions into the Indian country, and it seems probable that Gen. Terry would have participated in the campaign under any circumstances. Besides, it does not appear from Custer's despatch to Sheridan, that he had been promised more than the command of his regiment.

The history of the campaign, and the story of the disastrous battle in which Gen. Custer lost his life have been given in preceding chapters. His action in attacking the Indians before the arrival of Gibbon's troops has been the subject of controversy, and by some few even his motives have been impugned. The following paragraphs relative thereto are from the editorial columns of the *Army and Navy Journal*:

> It was not in Terry's instructions, and it clearly was not in his mind, that Custer, if he came "in contact with the enemy," should defer fighting him until the infantry came up. * * * There could be no justification whatever for any plan of operations which made an attack dependent upon a junction between Custer and Gibbon, after three or four days' march from different points.
>
> It has been asserted that, smarting under the wounds which preceding events had inflicted upon his pride, Custer dashed recklessly into this affair for the purpose of eclipsing his superior officers in the same field, regardless of cost or consequences. This, it seems to us, is going much too far. Custer was doubtless glad of the opportunity to fight the battle alone, and was stimulated by the anticipation of a victory which, illuminating his already brilliant career, would make him outshine those put on duty over him in this campaign. But his management of the affair was probably just about what it would have been under the same circumstances, if he had had no grievance. His great mistake was in acting in mingled ignorance of, and contempt for his enemy. He regarded attack and victory in this instance as synonymous terms, the only point being to prevent the escape of the foe. Under this fatal delusion he opened the engagement, with his command divided into four parts, with no certainty of co-operation or support between any two of them. Neither ambition, nor wounded vanity, prompted these vicious and fatal dispositions, nor were they due to lack of knowledge of the principles of his profession.

CHAPTER XIX

A BIOGRAPHICAL SKETCH OF MAJOR-GENERAL CUSTER (*concluded*)

As the foregoing biography of Gen. Custer has been confined chiefly to his military career, it may be well in conclusion to give some account of his personal characteristics; and this can be best done in the language of those who knew him well. A gentleman who accompanied Gen. Custer on the Yellowstone and Black Hills expeditions, contributed to the *New York Tribune* the following:

> Gen. Custer was a born cavalryman. He was never more in his element than when mounted on Dandy, his favorite horse, and riding at the head of his regiment. He once said to me, "I would rather be a private in the cavalry than a line officer in the infantry." He was the personification of bravery and dash. If he had only added discretion to his valor he would have been a perfect soldier. His impetuosity very often ran away with his judgment. He was impatient of control. He liked to act independently of others, and take all the risk and all the glory to himself. He frequently got himself into trouble by assuming more authority than really belonged to his rank. It was on the Yellowstone expedition where he came into collision with Gen. Stanley, his superior officer, and was placed under

arrest and compelled to ride at the rear of his column for two or three days, until Gen. Rosser, who fought against Custer in the Shenandoah Valley during the war but was then acting as engineer of the Northern Pacific Railroad, succeeded in effecting a reconciliation. Custer and Stanley afterward got on very well, and perhaps the quarrel would never have occurred if the two generals had been left alone to themselves without the intervention of camp gossips, who sought to foster the traditional jealousy between infantry and cavalry. For Stanley was the soul of generosity, and Custer did not really mean to be arrogant; but from the time when he entered West Point to the day when he fell on the Big Horn, he was accustomed to take just as much liberty as he was entitled to.

For this reason, Custer worked most easily and effectively when under general orders, when not hampered by special instructions, or his success made dependent on anybody else. Gen. Terry understood his man when, in the order directing him to march up the Rosebud, he very liberally said: "The Department Commander places too much confidence in your zeal, energy, and ability to wish to impose upon you precise orders which might hamper your action when nearly in contact with the enemy." But Gen. Terry did not understand Custer if he thought he would wait for Gibbon's support before attacking an Indian camp. Undoubtedly he ought to have done this; but with his native impetuosity, his reckless daring, his confidence in his own regiment, which had never failed him, and his love of public approval, Custer could no more help charging this Indian camp, than he could help charging just so many buffaloes. He had never learned to spell the word "defeat;" he knew nothing but success, and if he had met the Indians on the open plains, success would undoubtedly have been his; for no body of Indians could stand the charge of the 7th Cavalry when it swept over the Plains like a whirlwind. But in the Mauvaises Terres and the narrow valley of the Big Horn he did it at a fearful risk.

With all his bravery and self-reliance, his love of independent action, Custer was more dependent than most men on the kind approval of his fellows. He was even vain; he loved display in dress and in action. He would pay $40 for a pair of troop boots to wear on parade, and have everything else in keeping. On the Yellowstone expedition he wore a bright red shirt, which made him the best mark for a rifle of any man in the regiment. I remonstrated with him for this reckless exposure, but found an appeal to his wife more effectual, and on the next campaign he wore a buckskin suit. He formerly wore his hair very long, letting it fall in a heavy mass upon his shoulders, but cut it off before going out on the Black Hills, producing quite a change in his appearance. But if vain and ambitious, Custer had none of those great vices which are so common and so distressing in the army. He never touched liquor in any form; he did not smoke, or chew, or gamble. He was a man of great energy and remarkable endurance. He could outride almost any man in his regiment, I believe, if it were put to a test. When he set out to reach a certain point at a certain time, you could be sure that he would be there if he killed every horse in the command. He was sometimes too severe in forcing marches, but he never seemed to get tired himself, and he never expected his men to be so. In cutting our way through the forests of the Black Hills, I have often seen him take an ax and work as hard as any of the pioneers. He was never idle when he had a pretext for doing anything. Whatever he did he did thoroughly. He would overshoot the mark, but never fall short. He fretted in garrison sometimes, because it was too inactive; but he found an outlet here for his energies in writing articles for the press.

He had a remarkable memory. He could recall in its proper order every detail of any action, no matter how remote, of which he was a participant. He was rather verbose in writing, and had no gifts as a speaker; but his writings interested the masses from their close attention to details, and from his facility with the pen as with the sword in bringing a thing to a climax. As he was apt to overdo in action, so he was apt to exaggerate in statement, not from any wilful disregard of the truth, but because he saw things bigger than they really were. He did not distort the truth; he magnified it. He was a natural optimist. He took rose-colored views of everything, even of the miserable lands of the Northern Pacific Railroad. He had a historical memory, but not a historical mind. He was no philosopher; he could reel off facts from his mind better than he could analyze or mass them. He was not a student, nor a deep thinker. He loved to take part in events rather than to brood over them. He was fond of fun, genial and pleasant in his manner; a loving and devoted husband. It was my privilege to spend two weeks in his family at one time, and I know how happy he was in his social relations.

The following rambling remarks are accredited to a general, whose name is not given:

The truth about Custer is, that he was a pet soldier, who had risen not above his merit, but higher than men of equal merit. He fought with Phil Sheridan, and through the patronage of Sheridan he rose; but while Sheridan liked his valor and dash he never trusted his judgment. He was to Sheridan what Murat was to Napoleon. While Sheridan is always cool, Custer was always aflame. Rising to high command early in life, he lost the repose necessary to success in high command. * * * Then Custer must rush into politics, and went swinging around the circle with Johnson. He wanted to be a statesman, and but for Sheridan's influence with Grant, the republicans would have thrown him; but you see we all liked Custer, and did not mind his little freaks in that way any more than we would have minded temper in a woman. Sheridan, to keep Custer in his place, kept him out on the Plains at work. He gave him a fine command—one of the best cavalry regiments in the service.

The colonel, Sturgis, was allowed to bask in the sunshine in a large city, while Custer was the real commander. In this service Custer did well, and vindicated the partiality of Sheridan as well as the kind feelings of his friends. * * * The old spirit which sent Custer swinging around the circle revived in him. He came East and took a prominent part in reforming the army. This made feeling, and drew upon Custer the anger of the inside forces of the administration.

Then he must write his war memoirs. Well, in these memoirs he began to write recklessly about the army. He took to praising McClellan as the greatest man of the war, and, coming as it did when the democrats began to look lively, it annoyed the administration. Grant grew so much annoyed that even Sheridan could do no good, and Custer was disgraced. Technically it was not a disgrace. All that Grant did was to put Terry, a general, over Custer, a lieutenant-colonel, who had his regiment all the same; but all things considered, it was a disgrace.

The following is from an article by Gen. A. B. Nettleton, published in the *Philadelphia Times*:

It must be remembered that in fighting with cavalry, which was Custer's forte, instantaneous quickness of eye—that is, the lightning-like formation and execution of successive correct judgments on a rapidly-shifting situation—is the first thing, and the second is the power of inspiring the troopers with that impetuous yet intelligent ardor with which a mounted brigade becomes a thunderbolt, and without which it remains a useless, mass of horses and riders. These qualities Gen. Custer seemed to me to manifest, throughout the hard fighting of the last year of the war, to a degree that was simply astounding, and in a manner that marked him as one of the few really great cavalry commanders developed by the wars of the present century. Of fear, in the sense of dread of death or of bodily harm, he was absolutely destitute, yet his love of life and family and home was keen and constant, leaving no room in his nature for desperation, recklessness, or conscious rashness. In handling his division under Sheridan's general oversight, he seemed to act always on the belief that in campaigning with cavalry, when a certain work must be done, audacity is the truest caution. In action, when all was going well and success was only a question of time or of steady "pounding," Gen. Custer did not unnecessarily expose himself, but until the tide of battle had been turned in the right direction, and especially when disaster threatened, the foremost point in our division's line was almost invariably marked by the presence of Custer, his waving division tri-color and his plucky staff.

A major-general of wide and splendid fame at twenty-five, and now slain at thirty-six, the gallant Custer had already lived long if life be measured by illustrious deeds.

The following is from a sketch of Gen. Custer published in the *Army and Navy Journal*:

Custer was passionately addicted to active and exciting sports as the turf and hunting. He was a splendid horseman and a lover of the horse; he attended many American race-meetings and ran his own horses several times in the West. His greyhounds and staghounds went with him at the head of his regiment, to be let slip at antelope or buffalo. With rifle or shotgun he was equally expert, and had killed his grizzly bear in the most approved fashion. * * * Bold to rashness; feverish in camp, but cool in action; with the personal vanity of a carpet knight, and the endurance and insensibility to fatigue of the hardiest and boldest rough rider; a prince of scouts; a chief of guides, threading a trackless prairie with unerring eye of a native and the precision of the needle to the star; by no means a martinet, his men were led by the golden chain of love, admiration and confidence. He had the proverbial assurance of a hussar, but his personal appearance varied with occasion. During the war he was "Custer of the golden locks, his broad sombrero turned up from his hard-bronzed face, the ends of his crimson cravat floating over his shoulder, gold galore spangling his jacket sleeves, a pistol in his boot, jangling spurs on his heels, and a ponderous claymore swinging at his side." And long after, when he roamed a great Indian fighter on the Plains, the portrait was only slightly changed. The cavalry jacket was exchanged for the full suit of buckskin, beautifully embroidered by Indian maidens; across his saddle rested a modern sporting rifle, and at his horse's feet demurely walked hounds of unmixed breed. Again, within a few months, he appears in private society as an honored guest; scrupulously avoiding anything like display, but in a quiet conventional suit of blue, with the "golden locks" closely shorn, and the bronzed face pale from recent indisposition, he moves almost unnoticed in the throng.

The faithful correspondent who perished with Gen. Custer on the Little Big Horn portrayed him thus:

A man of strong impulses, of great hearted friendships and bitter enmities; of quick, nervous temperament, undaunted courage, will, and determination; a man possessing electric mental capacity, and of iron frame and constitution; a brave, faithful, gallant soldier, who has warm friends and bitter enemies; the hardest rider, the greatest pusher; with the most untiring vigilance overcoming seeming impossibilities, and with an ambition to succeed in all things he undertakes; a man to do right, as he construes right, in every case; one respected and beloved by his followers, who would freely follow him into the "jaws of hell."

Gen. Custer's last battle "will stand in history as one of the most heroic engagements ever fought, and his name will be respected so long as chivalry is applauded and civilization battles against barbarism."

CHAPTER XX

THE SIOUX TREATY OF 1876—INDIAN ORATORS

IN 1875, the Black Hills country had acquired a white population and an importance which rendered its possession and control by the Government desirable and necessary; and an attempt was made to treat with the Indians for its purchase, but without success.

In 1876, Congress expressed its determination to appropriate nothing more for the subsistence of the Sioux Indians unless they made certain concessions, including the surrender of the Black Hills, and entered into some agreement calculated to enable them to become self-supporting. Geo. W. Manypenny, H. C. Bullis, Newton Edmunds, Rt. Rev. H. B. Whipple, A. G. Boone, A. S. Gaylord, J. W. Daniels, and Gen. H. H. Sibley, were appointed commissioners to negotiate for the concessions demanded. The following is an extract from their instructions under which they acted:

> The President is strongly impressed with the belief that the agreement which shall be best calculated to enable the Indians to become self-supporting is one which shall provide for their removal, at as early

a day as possible, to the Indian Territory. For the past three years they have been kept from starvation by large appropriations for their subsistence. These appropriations have been a matter not of obligation but of charity, and the Indians should be made to understand distinctly that they can hope for continued appropriations only by full submission to the authority and wishes of the Government, and upon full evidence of their disposition to undertake, in earnest, measures for their own advancement and support.

The first council was held Sept. 7th, at Red Cloud agency, with chiefs and headmen representing 4,901 Indians then at the agency. Red Cloud and other chiefs met the commissioners with warm welcomes, and said with deep earnestness: "We are glad to see you; you have come to save us from death." The conditions required by Congress were then submitted to the Indians, with the assurance that the commissioners had no authority to change them in any particular; but that they were authorized to devise a plan to save their people from death and lead them to civilization. The plan decided on was then carefully explained and interpreted, and a copy of the agreement given to the Indians to take to their own council. Other councils were held Sept. 19th and 20th, and after mutual explanations the agreement was signed.

Subsequently, the commissioners visited Spotted Tail agency, Standing Rock agency, Cheyenne River agency, Crow Creek agency, Lower Brule agency, and Santee agency. At all of these agencies the agreement was made plain to the Indians, and after due deliberation and considerable discussion, duly signed. The following are extracts from the report of the commissioners:

> While the Indians received us as friends, and listened with kind attention to our propositions, we were painfully impressed with their lack of confidence in the pledges of the Government. At times they told their story of wrongs with such impassioned earnestness that our cheeks crimsoned with shame. In their speeches, the recital of the wrongs which their people had suffered at the hands of the whites, the arraignment of the Government for gross acts of injustice and fraud, the description of treaties made only to be broken, the doubts and distrusts of present professions of friendship and good-will, were portrayed in colors so vivid and language so terse, that admiration and surprise would have kept us silent had not shame and humiliation done so. Said a chief to a member of our commission: "I am glad to see you, you are our friends, but I hear that you have come to move us. Tell your people that since the Great Father promised that we should never be removed we have been moved five times." He added, with bitter irony, "I think you had better put the Indians on wheels so you can run them about wherever you wish."
>
> The present condition of the Sioux Indians is such as to awaken the deepest sympathy. They were our friends. If many of this powerful tribe have been changed to relentless foes, we must not forget that it is the simple outcome of our own Indian training-school. Generals Sherman, Harney, Terry, and others, use these words:
>
> "The moment the war of the rebellion was over, thousands of our people turned their attention toward the treasures of Montana. The Indian was forgotten. It did not occur to any man that this poor, despised red man was the original discoverer, and sole occupant for many centuries, of every mountain seamed with quartz and every stream whose yellow

sand glittered in the noonday sun. He asked to retain only a secluded spot where the buffalo and elk could live, and that spot he would make his home. The truth is, no place was left for him. If the lands of the white men are taken, civilization justifies him in resisting the invader. Civilization does more than this—it brands him as a coward and a slave if he submits to the wrong. If the savage resists, civilization, with the Ten Commandments in one hand and the sword in the other, demands his immediate extermination. That he goes to war is not astonishing. He is often compelled to do so. Wrongs are borne by him in silence that never fail to drive civilized men to deeds of violence. * * * But it is said that our wars with them have been almost constant. Have we been uniformly unjust? We answer unhesitatingly, 'yes.'"

General Stanley in 1870 writes from Dakota, that he is "ashamed to appear any longer in the presence of the chiefs of the different tribes of the Sioux, who inquire why we do not do as we promised, and in their vigorous language aver that we have lied." Sitting Bull, who had refused to come under treaty relations with the Government, based his refusal in these words, sent to the commission of which Assistant Secretary Cowen was chairman: "Whenever you have found a white man who will tell the truth, you may return, and I shall be glad to see you."

It has been claimed that all Indians found outside of their reservation shall be regarded as hostile. Gen. Sheridan, June 29th, 1869, says in an official order, that all Indians outside the well-defined limits of the reservation are under the original and exclusive jurisdiction of the military authority, *and as a rule will be considered hostile.* This order is the more surprising to us when we remember that the treaty made by General Sherman and others expressly provided that these Indians might hunt upon the unceded territory; and we find that so late as its last session Congress appropriated $200,000 to be used in part for the payment of the seventh of thirty installments "*for Indians roaming.*" We repeat that, under this treaty, it is expressly provided that the Indians may hunt in the unceded territory north and west of the Sioux reservation, and until last year they had the right to hunt in Western Nebraska. We believe that our failure to recognize this right has led to many conflicts between the citizens and army of the United States and the Indians.

In 1874, the late lamented Gen. Custer made an expedition to the Black Hills. It was done against the protest of the Indians and their friends, and in plain, direct violation of the treaty. Gold was discovered, white men flocked to the El Dorado. Notwithstanding the gross violation of the treaty, no open war ensued. If our own people had a sad story of wrongs suffered from the Indians, we must not forget that the Indians, who own no telegraph-lines, who have no press and no reporters, claimed that they, too, had been the victims of lawless violence, and had a country of untold value wrested from them by force.

The charge is made that the agency Indians are hostile, and that they have furnished ammunition and supplies to the Indians with Sitting Bull. There is water-navigation for 3,000 miles through this territory, and an unguarded border of several hundred miles along the Canadian frontier. So long as the Indians will sell buffalo-robes at a low price and pay two prices for guns, the greed of white men will furnish them. It is gross injustice to the agents and the Interior Department to accuse them of furnishing arms and ammunition for Indians to fight our army and murder our citizens.

Of the results of this year's war we have no wish to speak. It is a heart-rending record of the slaughter of many of the bravest of our army. It has not only carried desolation and woe to hundreds of our own hearthstones, but has added to the cup of anguish which we have pressed to the lips of the Indian. We fear that when others shall examine it in the light of history, they will repeat the words of the officers who penned the report of 1868: "The results of the year's campaign satisfied all reasonable men that the war was useless and expensive."

We hardly know how to frame in words the feelings of shame and sorrow which fill our hearts as we recall the long record of the broken faith of our Government. It is made more sad, in that the rejoicings of our centennial year are mingled with the wail of sorrow of widows and orphans made by a needless Indian war, and that our Government has expended more money in this war than all the religious bodies of our country have spent in Indian missions since our existence as a nation.

After long and careful examination we have no hesitation in recommending that it is wise to continue the humane policy inaugurated by President Grant. The great obstacle to its complete success is that no change has been made in the laws for the care of Indians. The Indian is left without the protection of law in person, or property, or life. He has no personal rights. He has no redress for wrongs inflicted by lawless violence. He may see his crops destroyed, his wife or child killed. His only redress is personal revenge. * * * In the Indian's wild state he has a rude government of chiefs and headmen, which is advisory in its character. When located upon reservations under the charge of a United States agent, this government is destroyed, and we give him nothing in its place.

We are aware that many of our people think that the only solution of the Indian problem is in their extermination. We would remind such persons that there is only One who can exterminate. There are too many graves within our borders over which the grass has hardly grown, for us to forget that God is just. The Indian is a savage, but he is also a man. He is one of the few savage men who clearly recognize the existence of a Great Spirit. He believes in the immortality of the soul. He has a passionate love for his children. He loves his country. He will gladly die for his tribe. Unless we deny all revealed religion, we must admit that he has the right to share in all the benefits of divine revelation. He is capable of civilization. Amid all the obstacles, the wrongs, and evils of our Indian policy, there are no missions which show richer rewards. Thousands of this poor race, who were once as poor and degraded as the wild Sioux, are today civilized men, living by the cultivation of the soil, and sharing with us in those blessings which give to men home, country, and freedom. There is no reason why these men may not also be led out of darkness to light.

The following is a synopsis of the arrangement agreed on by the commissioners and Indians:

The Sioux surrender all claim to so much of their reservation as lies west of the 103d meridian of longitude, and to so much of it as lies between the North and South Forks of the Cheyenne River east of said meridian; also all claim to any country lying outside of their reservation. Cannon Ball River and its south branch are to be the northern boundary of the reservation. Three wagon or other roads may be maintained across the reservation from the Missouri River to the Black Hills. All subsistence and supplies which may be hereafter provided, are to be delivered on or near the Missouri River. A delegation of chiefs and leading men from each band shall visit the Indian Territory, with a view to selecting therein a permanent home for the Indians. If such delegation shall make a selection satisfactory to the Indians they represent and to the United States, then the Indians are to remove to the selected country within one year, select allotments as soon as possible afterwards, and use their best efforts to cultivate the same. They are in all things to submit themselves to such beneficent plans as the Government may provide for them in the selection of a permanent home where they may live like white men.

The United States agree to furnish subsistence to the Sioux until such time as they shall become self-supporting—rations to be issued to heads of families; and in case the Indians are located on lands suitable for cultivation, and educational facilities are afforded by the Government, the issue of rations is to be conditioned on the performance of labor by the Indians and the attendance of their children at school. Assistance in the way of schools and instruction in the agricultural and mechanical arts, as provided by the treaty of 1868, is guaranteed; and the building of comfortable houses on allotments in severalty is provided for. The Sioux are declared amenable to the laws of the United States; and Congress shall secure to them an orderly government and protect individual property, person, and life. The agreement not to be binding on either party till approved by Congress and the President.

With the exception of the Santees, the Indians on the Missouri River objected to visiting the Indian Territory, and were exempted from that part of the agreement by a supplementary clause. A delegation of 90 Indians from the Red Cloud and Spotted Tail agencies visited the Indian Territory in October as provided in the agreement. The following is from the report of Commissioners Boone and Daniels who accompanied the delegation:

While travelling through the Territory, Spotted Tail took special pains to inform us that he was not pleased with anything that came within his observation, and his part of the delegation, with but few exceptions, were not disposed to express themselves in any other way. Many of the Red Cloud party were well pleased. Their chief said "his Great Father asked him to go and find a place where his children could live by cultivating the land. This was the country, and he should go back and tell his people so." The manual-labor school of 120 scholars at the Cheyenne and Arapahoe agency, was of more interest to them and gave them more pleasure than anything else seen on the journey. They manifested much interest in the progress of civilization among the Sac and Fox, and when passing the Creek country, the delegation was received by these tribes with generous hospitality and a hearty welcome. When we were at Okmulgee, the capital of the Creek Nation, they were invited to the council-house by the Creek chief, where he made a very friendly speech to them. The following is a copy thereof:

"To the Sioux, my brethren: I am well pleased to see you here in the Mus-koke Nation, brethren of the same race as ourselves. I was told a long time ago of my red brethren, the Sioux, that were living in the far Northwest. I had heard of the name of your tribe and of many of your leading chiefs. I have heard of your great men, great in war, and great in council. I have heard of your trouble on account of the intrusion of the white men on your reservation in search of gold. I have heard that the United States Government had determined to remove you from your present home, and, perhaps it might be, to this Indian Territory, to the west of us. When I heard that you might possibly come to this Territory, which has been 'set apart for the home of the Indians forever,' I was glad. I would like to have all our red brethren settled in this Territory, as we have provided in our treaty. We, the Creeks and Cherokees, have the same kind of title and patent for our lands from the United States, which guarantees this Territory to us for a home, under our own form of government, by people of our own race, as long as 'grass grows and water runs.' And I think, therefore, we shall live forever on our lands. I should like—and I express the wish of our people—that every Indian tribe should come here and settle on these lands, that this Territory may become filled up with Indians, to the exclusion of others who may be inimical to our race and interests. We believe our right to our soil and our government, which is best suited to our peculiar necessities, would be safer if all our race were united together here. This is my earnest wish. Then I think the rising generation could be educated and civilized, and, what is still better, christianized, which, I believe, would be the greatest benefit of all. This would be to our mutual benefit and good. I know I express the minds of our people when I give you this welcome to our life of a higher civilization, which is better than the old life so long led by our race in the past."

At the councils held at the different agencies, the chiefs and principal men made numerous speeches, which conveyed a good idea of Indian views and feelings, and were often able and eloquent. The balance of this chapter will be filled up with extracts from some of these speeches.

Red Cloud Agency. FAST BEAR: My good friends, you have come here to ask me for something, and I have come here to-day to answer. You ask me to give up the mountains that are to the north of us, and I answer yes to that question. I give them up. You are here also to ask me to take a journey to look at a country, and I also answer yes to that question. I consent for my young men to go down there and see that country; but they must look at it in silence, and come back in silence. When they have seen the country I will consider it. If it is good I will consider it so; if bad I will consider that it is bad. Do you understand, my friends, what I last said to you? We do not agree to go there to live before we have seen the country.

YOUNG-MAN-AFRAID-OF-HIS-HORSE: My father shook hands with the Dakotas peacefully on the Platte River. I have been brought up here from a boy until I got to be a chief. The soldiers have no business in this country at all. I wish to tell you plainly that I have been very much ashamed ever since the soldiers came here. This is my country, and I have remained here with my women and children eating such things as the Great Father has sent us. I am going to ask the Great Father for a great many things, things that will make me rich. I am going to ask for so much that I am afraid the Great Father will not consent to give it to me. I want you to tell the Great Father that I, and all the men like me, and the children, are going to ask him for a great many things, and we expect to have food, and blankets to wear as long as we live.

BLACK COAL: This place here is a place of peace, where we and our people have lived together happily, and behaved ourselves, and we do not understand why so many soldiers have come here among us. We have never had any trouble and have behaved ourselves, and wish to have the soldiers sent away as soon as possible, and leave us in peace. The people that live here have both minds and hearts and good sense, but it seems as if the Great Father all at once thought differently, and speaks of us as people that are very bad.

RED CLOUD: The commissioners have both brains and hearts. The Great Father has sent you here to visit me and my people, and I want that you should help us. We see a great many soldiers here in our country. We do not like to see them here. I want you to have pity upon us, and have them all taken away. I understand all the ways of the whites. I know that everything that has been said has been written down, and I should like to have a fair copy of that made and given to me.

LITTLE WOUND: I always considered that when the Great Father borrowed the country for the overland road that he made an arrangement with us that was to last fifty years as payment for that privilege, and yesterday another arrangement was mentioned concerning the Black Hills, and the words that I heard from the Great Father and from the commissioners from the Great Council made me cry. The country upon which I am standing is the country upon which I was born, and upon which I heard that it was the wish of the Great Father and of the Great Council that I should be like a man without a country. I shed tears. I wish that the chief men among you that have come here to see me would help me, and would change those things that do not suit me.

Spotted Tail Agency. SPOTTED TAIL: My friends that have come here to see me; you have brought to us words from the Great Father at Washington, and I have considered them now for seven days, and have made up my mind. This is the fifth time that you have come. At the time of the first treaty that was made on Horse Creek—the one we call the "great treaty"—there was provision made to borrow the overland road of the Indians, and promises made at the time of the treaty, though I was a boy at the time; they told me it was to last fifty years. These promises have not been kept. All the words have proved to be false. The next conference was the one held with Gen. Manydear [Maynadier], when there were no promises made in particular, nor for any amount to be given to us, but we had a conference with him and made friends and shook hands. Then after that there was a treaty made by Gen. Sherman. He told us we should have annuities and goods from that treaty for thirty-five years. He said this, but yet he didn't tell the truth. He told me the country was mine, and that I should select any place I wished for my reservation and live in it. My friends, I will show you well his words to-day. * * * I see that my friends before me are men of age and dignity. I think that each of you have selected somewhere a good piece of land for himself, with the intention of living on it, that he may there raise up his children. My people, that you see here before you, are not different; they also live upon the earth and upon the things that come to them from above.

My friends, this seems to me to be a very hard day, and we have come upon very difficult times. This war did not spring up here in our land; this war was brought upon us by the children of the Great Father who came to take our land from us without price, and who, in our land, do a great many evil things. We have a store-house to hold our provisions the Great Father sends us, but he sends very little provisions to put in our store-house. When our people become displeased with their provisions and have gone north to hunt in order that they might live, the Great Father's children are fighting them. It has been our wish to live in our country peaceably, but the Great Father has filled it with soldiers who think only of our death. It seems to me there is a better way than this. When people come to trouble, it is better for both parties to come together without arms and talk it over and find some peaceful way to settle it. My friends, you have come to me to-day, and mentioned two countries to me. One of them I know of old—the Missouri River. It is not possible for me to go there. When I was there before we had a great deal of trouble. I left also 100 of my people buried there. The other country you have mentioned is one I have never seen since I was born, but I agree to go and look at it. When men have a difficult business to settle it is not possible it should be well settled in one day; it takes at least twelve months to consider it.

Spotted Tail: (*Second Council.*) This war has come from robbery—from the stealing of our land. My friends, I wish to tell the Great Father "Let us consider this matter." There are on both sides a great many widows and a great many orphans. Let us consider who is to take care of these. This matter has not been begun with judgment; and I think it is displeasing to the Great Spirit. The Great Father sent you out here to buy our land and we have agreed together to that, but with one understanding: That it shall be the end, also, of this war. We have always been peaceful friends of the Great Father, and shall remain at peace with him; but all at once a whirlwind has passed over our land, and the ammunition has been locked up so that we cannot get it to hunt game to live upon. Now we shake hands and make peace and wish it to be unlocked so we can buy ammunition. You know this trouble does not please the Great Spirit, and I want you to help me to blot it out.

Baptiste Good: You have come here with considerations that will make my people live, and my heart is glad. When Gen. Sherman came to make a treaty with my people, I was also glad. That was like the birth of a child. I wish you would tell the Great Father we need implements to work with, and wagons for two horses. I have worn out my fingers working without implements. I have planted corn, and I am happy to say it has grown up and produced fruit. The white minister has come here to teach me, but I don't think it is done properly. I would like to have some female ministers come dressed in black to receive the girls in one house and teach them, and have white male ministers in black hat and coat to teach the boys in another house separately.

Blue Teeth: Just such men as you came to make the treaty with me. They showed me a road to walk in, and I showed my people and advised them according to their words, and they were glad. But the things they promised me didn't turn out as they promised them. I am the man that heard the promises made. Spotted Tail told you about that yesterday, according to my direction, but I was hiding myself. I want the man pointed out that is going to talk to the Great Father. [Judge Gaylord is pointed out.] You see that pipe: take it, [handing to Judge Gaylord a pipe and tobacco-pouch.] The Great Spirit gave me that pipe. He told me to point it to my mother, the earth, when I prayed. I wish you to take it to the Great Father at Washington, and tell him a man that made a speech here presented it to him, and ask him to be merciful to him and help him to live. Tell him this is my country, and for him to have pity upon me and not move me away from it. I want to live here always.

Standing Rock Agency. John Grass: Look well at me with both eyes and listen to me with both ears. I have considered the words you have brought me, and I am ready to answer you. The chiefs you see here have all come to the same conclusion. You have brought words to the chiefs here that will bring life to their children; that will make their children live; they answer *how* [signifying their approval] to that. And now since they have ceded their country to you, they want to tell you of certain things that they shall want in the future.

RUNNING ANTELOPE: When people shake hands and talk, they talk in earnest. I want you to look on this man Kill Eagle, with his people who are prisoners here. He is one of us and is our kindred. Kindred living with each other love each other, and when they get into trouble they help each other out, and we look on these Indians the same as white. He went out to the hostile camp, held his gun, witnessed a fight, and came back. I want before the sun sets to see these men released. I am an old man, and I ask these things as a favor.

In regard to this store. I have been to see the Great Father, and the white people are wealthy. Even they have stores one right against the other, touching each other. When a man goes in a store and finds something he wants and cannot obtain it as cheaply as he desires, he goes into another, and so on until he gets what he wants and at the proper price. We want to do so here.

TWO BEARS: Hail Great Spirit, and hail my friends who I see here, and hail Great Father! My heart is this day made glad by seeing you here. You prayed to the Great Spirit and that made our hearts glad. I was the chief owner of this country, but the Great Father turned it over to his young men. This was a hard thing for him to do to me; now that he proposes to pay me for it I am very glad. I am of the fifth generation of the Sioux Indians, and the sixth generation is growing up around me. I want the Government to provide for the same number of generations in the future. I am making this trade with the Great Father, and I am not a white man and am not able to live like a white man. They eat but little, but I am not able to get along with a little yet. The Great Spirit fed me, and fed me in large quantities. I eat all day, and eating great quantities has become a habit with me. I am afraid of frightful things; I am afraid of bad things; I am afraid of a battle. I like good things, and straightforward dealings. For two winters I was starving and have eaten a great number of my horses and dogs. In consequence of this starvation many of our people fled from the agency in search of food, and while they were out one of them got into trouble. [referring to Kill Eagle.]

Mad Bear: I am an Indian, a poor, miserable Indian, but if I should do as has been done by us, the Great Spirit would dislike, and hate me, and for that reason I cannot do these things. Men, civilians, that we have had for agents would steal our food, steal things that were sent to us. It is the fault of the white men that this is done. They select men that belong to the ring. When one agent is removed they select his friend to succeed him, and so the stealing goes on. The matter of their traders alone is enough to drive the Indians hostile. It would drive a white man hostile to be treated as we are treated, and to be charged prices as our traders charge us for goods. If an Indian succeeds in getting a dollar he takes it to the store to trade, and what he receives in return for it amounts to probably half a dime. We want the monopoly of trading stores stopped. The work, the labor, everything is monopolized by white men, who have everything their own way. It is hard to be an Indian chief. Our young men do not listen to us—they will not mind us.

Fool Dog: The Great Spirit created these men and they expect to raise children after them. Generations are not to stop here, they are still to go on living, and we look to you for help and assistance. I am an Indian, and am looked on by the whites as a foolish man; but it must be because I follow the advice of the white man.

Long Soldier: The Great Spirit called me forth to be a chief, and this day I say *how* to you. The Great Father has asked me for a portion of my country and has made me an offer in return for it. I am very glad to get what has been offered to me, and I therefore say *how* to your proposition. I am a very suspicious man and always suspect people of some evil designs when they talk to me, and therefore remain at home. My father, who has instructed me to be a friend of the whites, is still living, and I want him to share in the benefits that arise from the sale of the Black Hills.

Two Bears: My friends, to-day we have talked together with smiles on our faces, and we are going to sign this paper with the understanding that everything in it is true, and that we are not deceiving each other. My children are very poor and very ignorant, and they don't know anything about weights and measures, and if you are going to issue my rations by weight I want you to give good measure. In signing this agreement I don't sign it myself; I have a young man who is my hope for the future. Although I touch the pen myself, I touch it for my son, who is to be my successor.

Drag Wood: I am an old man and my bones are getting sore, and I want my son to sign this agreement with me.

Wolf Necklace: I never want to leave this country; all my relatives are lying here in the ground, and when I fall to pieces I am going to fall to pieces here.

Cheyenne River Agency. Long Mandan: I am glad of one thing; the Great Father knows that this is my country, and before he takes it from me he is going to ask my permission. Our people are poor, they have nothing in their lodges, and if you will visit them you would feel disposed to bring many things to them to-day. My friends, when I went to Washington I went into your money-house, and I had some young men with me, but none of them took any money out of that house while I was with them. At the same time, when your Great Father's people come into my country, they go into my money-house and take money out.

More than that, they commit depredations on us; and stole fifty head of horses and took them away from me. If the Great Father was not a great man and was not a man that had great power and a good man, I should have been mad; but he is a great man and a good man, and that is the reason that I have not been offended at him. I would much rather have gone to Washington with my people and have signed this treaty there. I do not want to spend a great deal of money for the Great Father, but at the same time I know that the Great Father is wealthy. I want to tap the telegraph that is over the river, and talk to the Great Father in that way, and to have him answer me in the same way. I want him to give me plenty of mowing-machines, and I would like very much to have a good blacksmith. I will show you something to-day that I have done in this country in the way of farming; a large pumpkin that I have sent to be brought here to show you. My friends, you may think that I never raised it when you see it, but I want to show it to you, and have sent for it.

RED FEATHER: The Great Father asked me in regard to the missions and churches and schools, and told me I must take hold of that and assist him. There were two ministers here, and I regarded them as two canes to walk upon and help me up with. There is one thing that the people of the Great Father have that I do not want, and that is whisky. I do not want any whisky on my reservation. Whenever a man drinks whisky he loses his senses, and that is the reason why I object to it.

DUCK: The soldiers that are fighting have killed a great many people on both sides, and have made many widows and orphans on both sides. I am sorry to know that anybody was killed on either side. All the badness and all the trouble that has occurred here formerly, I gather it up in my hand and throw it away; tell the Great Father that. Look at this people; they are poor people; they have a hard time to get what little furs and hides they have; but when we take them to the stores we do not get enough for them. If you are not afraid of me, and do not think I am fooling with you, I would like to have you attend to this hide business, and see that we get $6 apiece for them.

White Bull: I see, my friends, the soldiers standing here about me. They are people whose business it is to die, but we think better things for them. We have given them the Black Hills; we wish they would go there and dig gold without being afraid of anybody.

Crow Creek Agency. White Ghost: Around and about the hills on the prairies there are a great many dead people lying, but the Great Father has decided to give us a good price for the hills; therefore it is—because the Great Father is strong—that we are willing to give them up. We live right near a trading post, and we become poor because we have not money to buy those things we want. I do not wish you to think that I am finding fault or out of temper. I merely say the things I am instructed to say. My people wish to have it understood that they do not wish to have any soldiers sent here or any soldier for an agent. I must tell everything that I am instructed to say; they are all here listening to see whether I say everything, and I must say all that I have been told. We would like to have Mr. Premeau appointed for interpreter. He is a white man, a man that understands the language, and does not drink whisky. My people think that the flour that is sent here for them is sent for them to eat, and they are not pleased that it is fed to the pigs about the agency; and they wish me to mention that we take a hide to the store, quite a large one, and receive an order for three dollars' worth of goods. For this large beef-hide we get one piece of leather the width of three fingers, for a belt; it is not worth more than fifty cents. That does not please us.

Last summer when I went to the council for the Black Hills, I had a pipe with me. I told them, in reference to the Black Hills, that we were bound by giving and receiving the pipe, the same as white people when they make an oath in court and swear upon the Bible, and if the party took the pipe that was offered to him in council and held it in his hand everything went well, and if he did not speak the truth always some evil would spring up in connection with it. Last summer the pipe was given in council, and what do you think of the matter now? Have the promises been kept, or has the violation of them caused war and bloodshed? I have for a long time known the ways of your people in dealing with us and taking away our country, and I know that they have been such as to make us miserable. You have driven away our game and our means of livelihood out of the country, until now we have nothing left that is valuable except the hills that you ask us to give up. When we give these up to the Great Father we know that we give up the last thing that is valuable either to us or the white people; and therefore my people wish me to say that, as long as two Indians are living, we expect them to have the benefit of the price paid for these lands.

My friend, [to the chairman,] I am going to give you a pipe. Perhaps we are deceiving each other in this matter, perhaps we are not going to be truthful, and shall commit a great sin, but I for my part am trying to speak the truth.

Running Bear: I look upon you as you sit before me, and I see that there are no boys among you; that you are all men of age, and I am glad to see it. I am very old, very near the time when I shall lie down in the earth. Therefore if you have really come to help us we are very happy. I will speak now about myself. I am an orphan. Before my father died he told me that my country was very valuable. You say you are going to give me rations by weight; I do not know anything about that; I think it will take me at least twelve years to understand it. It is only yesterday that the people of my generation were laid in the ground, and I am the only one left. My father, who is now dead, went to the Great Father's house and talked with him there. The people have now given you the Black Hills, and we for our part would like to go to our Great

Father's house and hear how much money he proposes to give us in return. Again, the whisky that the white people have and carry about with them is very bad. We hear that our people who are living up to the north of us drink a great deal of whisky. We do not like it at all. My friends, I am going to ask you for something that I want. I do not think it possible that you have come out here to ask me for something without paying me for it. I do not consider myself very rich. You white people come out here with a great many pockets in your clothes. Probably the person who sent you told you what to do with the things in your pockets. I would like to have you take up a collection. Each of you put your hands in your pockets and take out ten cents and give it to me to buy something at the store. You are not particularly modest in asking for the things you want, and I see no reason why I should not ask for the things that I want. Do you think I do right in asking you?

You are a chief, [to the chairman.] I, also, am a chief. I have lived here now 13 years. I do not remember even a bad word that I have said; perhaps the Great Father does. In every country there are men who are skillful in talking in council. I am such a man myself. I also have been instructed. This medal that you see, was put about my neck by a Catholic priest, and yet, notwithstanding I am so honored, you talk to me about issuing rations by weight. I am astonished at you. You are advanced in years; I am also advanced in years.

White Bear: I wonder if you know that I planted a field out here. I raised pumpkins as large as this chair and corn taller than I am, and after I had done that my father took my field away to plant oats in. I wonder if you know that. Tell the Great Father that there is only one store here, and all the young men are shedding tears about it. If they had mowing-machines, such as they could ride upon, to ride around their country and cut hay, they would be able to earn something; but the agent considers that the country belongs to him personally, and cuts all the hay. My friends, I would like to have our agent, before the sun goes down, climb up into the second story of the warehouse and take down all the teepee cloths and blankets that he has there, and divide them among the people.

DOG BACK: I am not anybody in particular. Although I am not very strong and a man of no special importance, I took a claim, and planted, and considered that I was watching my own hay and grass. I am the man that has been trying to live in the way that I have been told, but this summer a great many white men have come there and cut my wood, and killed the fowls and animals I have raised, and disturbed me in many ways. I do not wish to make any disturbance about it, but I have been trying to do as the Great Father advised us, and it seems to me that these people who come and do such things to me are lawless people. I have nobody to help me, but you come here to-day from the Great Father, and I have told you these things in the hope that you will help me.

Santee Agency. HAKEWASTE: I am an Indian and was born naked. I now wear the same kind of clothes as the white man. Old Wabashaw told me that the President wanted us to work, and for that reason I have dressed in this way, but what you have been explaining to me I know nothing about. I have only been six years a chief in this land. You can see how we are situated here; that we have done part of what the President told us to do; you see little patches of corn, &c. As old man Wabashaw is buried here we would all like to live here. We will all do what you ask of us in the treaty. We own nothing, and have nothing to depend upon. When the President makes up his mind to do a thing he generally does it, but we do not want to go to that territory to the south.

WAMAMSA: The Lord above rules everything, and he has given us a nice mild day for our council. We have prayed for land and churches, and as we now have three churches I think the Lord has taken good care of us and has answered our prayers. Look at these young men. You have not seen any Indians during your travels dressed in that way. We are not getting along very well—not as well as we should. Twice now we have had Quakers for agents, and we are going down hill all the time; getting into the ground.

HUSASA: I have been blind for four years, but I can hear what is said. When any one comes from Washington to see us we ought to be thankful to him. When we lived at Redwood we made the treaty, and it was mentioned that we were to draw annuities and money for fifty years, and for that reason we put ourselves in the wrong place and suffer for it to-day. There are only three chiefs left now, and all we have to do is to throw ourselves into the arms of the Great Father. We are all pretty badly off. When people used to come here from Washington, Wabashaw was here to speak, but now he is lying in the ground and we are all the time looking that way at him. A great many of us have no wagons or oxen or anything to work with. I have nothing but an old wagon that is not fit for use, and am as poor as if I had not sold any land to the President. The Indians' minds are not very long and we forget a thing in a very short time. You have told us what to do. We have got it all in our ears and ought to be proud of it.

The President said that he would take good care of us, and now here I am blind and have not got a wagon fit to use. Although I am blind, if I had a wagon the women or some of the boys could bring me water when I am thirsty.

INDEX